VOGUE KNITTING

VINTAGE KNITS

VOGUE KNITTING

VINTAGE KNITS

THE BUTTERICK® PUBLISHING COMPANY
NEW YORK

THE BUTTERICK® PUBLISHING COMPANY
161 Avenue of the Americas
New York, New York 10013

THE BUTTERICK® PUBLISHING COMPANY and colophon
are registered trademarks of Butterick® Company, Inc.

Library of Congress Cataloging-in-Publication Data

Vogue knitting vintage knits/ [editor-in-chief, Trisha Malcolm].
p. cm. – (Vogue knitting on the go!)
ISBN 1-57389-026-X (alk. paper)
1. Knitting–Patterns. I. Title: Vintage Knits. II. Malcolm, Trisha, 1960- III. Series.

TT825 .V649 2000
746.43'20432–dc21   00-064176

Manufactured in China

1 3 5 7 9 10 8 6 4 2

First Edition

TABLE OF CONTENTS

INTRODUCTION

Remember when life moved at a slower pace and people took the time to create beautiful things for themselves and their families? Take knitting for example—making a garment requires time, effort, and patience; buying off the rack just involves a trip to the mall or a click of the mouse. Yes, it's more convenient, but isn't it equally satisfying (if not more so) to create something beautiful and enduring with your own two hands?

Here's your chance to recapture that feeling of accomplishment. From the refined elegance of the 1930s to the sassy chic of the 1960s, the patterns in this book span four decades of great style and great knitting. Each project is a classic worth revisiting and an item that will find a place in your wardrobe (or the next generation's!) for years to come.

Make time to knit. It's a wonderful stress reliever and it's easier than you think. Work a few rows on your morning commute, while sitting in the stands at your child's soccer game or during a class lecture—maybe even slip in a stitch or two while you wait for that Web page to download! With each click of the needles, stress will melt away.

Put the modern world on hold for a while and get ready to **KNIT ON THE GO!**

THE BASICS

Hand-knitting has endured throughout the centuries as a loving and meaningful expression for both the knitter and the fortunate recipient. From the simplest repetitive patterns to the wizardry of stitch and color complexities, knitting offers a lifetime of challenges and pleasures.

Vogue Knitting magazine has always presented up-to-the-minute fashion looks with a sense of pride and satisfaction. With this spirit in mind, *Vintage Knits* takes a journey back in time to bring you this comprehensive collection of styles spanning the 1930s through the 1960s. Current yarns, along with simple and concise instructions, have updated each project for a fresh, modern look to complement the original lines.

Whether you are searching for a timeless sweater or an accessory for yourself, a new baby gift or a unique treasure for a member of your family, you can expect to find the perfect pattern in this outstanding collection of vintage knits.

SIZING

Since clothing measurements have changed in recent decades, it is important to measure yourself or a sweater that fits well, to determine which size to make.

YARN SELECTION

For an exact reproduction of the projects photographed, use the yarn listed in the "Materials" section of the pattern. We've chosen yarns that are readily available in the U.S. and Canada at the time of printing. The Resources list on pages 86 and 87 provides addresses of yarn distributors. Contact them for the name of a retailer in your area.

YARN SUBSTITUTION

You may wish to substitute yarns. Perhaps you view small-scale projects as a chance to incorporate leftovers from your yarn stash, or the yarn specified may not be available in your area. You'll need to knit to the given gauge to obtain the knitted measurements with a substitute yarn (see "Gauge" on page 11). Be sure to consider how the fiber content of the substitute yarn will affect the comfort and the ease of care of your projects.

To facilitate yarn substitution, *Vogue Knitting* grades yarn by the standard stitch gauge obtained in stockinette stitch. You'll find a grading number in the "Materials" section of the pattern, immediately following the fiber type of the yarn. Look for a substitute yarn that falls into the same category. The suggested needle size and gauge on the ball band should be comparable to that on the Yarn Symbols chart (see page 18).

After you've successfully gauge-swatched a substitute yarn, you'll need to figure out how much of the substitute yarn the project requires. First, find the total length of the original yarn in the pattern (multiply number of balls by

GAUGE

It is always important to knit a gauge swatch, and it is even more so with garments to ensure proper fit.

Patterns usually state gauge over a 4"/10cm span, however it's beneficial to make a larger test swatch. This gives a more precise stitch gauge, a better idea of the appearance and drape of the knitted fabric, and gives you a chance to familiarize yourself with the stitch pattern.

The type of needles used—straight- or double-pointed, wood or metal—will influence gauge, so knit your swatch with the needles you plan to use for the project. Measure gauge as illustrated. Try different needle sizes until your sample measures the required number of stitches and rows. *To get fewer stitches to the inch/cm, use larger needles; to get more stitches to the inch/cm, use smaller needles.*

Knitting in the round may tighten the gauge, so if you measured the gauge on a flat swatch, take another gauge reading after you begin knitting. When the piece measures at least 2"/5cm, lay it flat and measure over the stitches in the center of the piece, as the side stitches may be distorted.

It's a good idea to keep your gauge swatch in order to test blocking and cleaning methods.

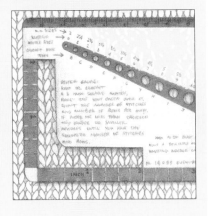

yards/meters per ball). Divide this figure by the new yards/meters per ball (listed on the ball band). Round up to the next whole number. The answer is the number of balls required.

FOLLOWING CHARTS

Charts are a convenient way to follow colorwork, lace, cable, and other stitch patterns at a glance. *Vogue Knitting* stitch charts utilize the universal knitting language of "symbolcraft." When knitting back and forth in rows, read charts from right to left on right side (RS) rows and from left to right on wrong side (WS) rows, repeating any stitch and row repeats as directed in the pattern. When knitting in the round, read charts from right to left on every round. Posting a self-adhesive note under your working row is an easy way to keep track of your place on a chart.

LACE

Lace knitting provides a feminine touch. Knitted lace is formed with "yarn overs," which create an eyelet hole in combination with decreases that create directional effects to make a yarn over (yo), merely pass the yarn over the right-hand needle to form a new loop. Decreases are worked as k2tog, ssk, or SKP depending on the desired slant and are spelled out specifically with each instruction. On the row or round that follows the lace or eyelet detail, each yarn over is treated as one stitch. If you're new to lace knitting, it's a good idea to count the stitches at the end of each row or round. Making a gauge swatch in the stitch pattern enables you to practice the lace pattern. Instead of binding off the swatch, place the final row on a holder, as the bind off tends to pull in the stitches and distort the gauge.

COLORWORK KNITTING

Two main types of colorwork are explored in this book.

INTARSIA

Intarsia is accomplished with separate bobbins of individual colors. This method is ideal for large blocks of color or for motifs that aren't repeated close together. When changing colors, always pick up the new color and wrap it around the old color to prevent holes.

For smaller areas of color, such as the accent diamonds on the Woman's Argyle Anklet (page 56), duplicate stitch embroidery is done after the pieces are knit.

STRANDING

When motifs are closely placed, colorwork is accomplished by stranding along two or more colors per row, creating "floats" on the wrong side of the fabric. This technique is sometimes called Fair Isle knitting after the traditional Fair Isle patterns that are composed of small motifs with frequent color changes.

To keep an even tension and prevent holes while knitting, pick up yarns alternately over and under one another across or around. While knitting, stretch the stitches on the needle slightly wider than the length of the float at the back to keep work from puckering.

When changing colors at the beginning of rows or rounds, carry yarn along for a few rows only, or cut yarn and rejoin when needed. It is important to keep the "floats" small and neat so they don't catch when pulling on the piece.

BLOCKING

Blocking is an all-important finishing step in the knitting process. It is the best way to shape pattern pieces and smooth knitted edges in preparation for sewing together. Most garments retain their shape if the blocking stages in the instructions are followed carefully. Choose a blocking method according the the yarn care label and when in doubt, test-block your gauge swatch.

WET BLOCK METHOD

Using rust-proof pins, pin pieces to measurements on a flat surface and lightly dampen using a spray bottle. Allow to dry before removing pins.

STEAM BLOCK METHOD

With WS facing, pin pieces. Steam lightly, holding the iron 2"/5cm above the knitting. Do not press or it will flatten stitches.

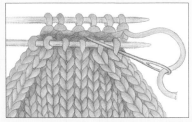

1 Insert tapestry needle purlwise (as shown) through first stitch on front needle. Pull yarn through, leaving that stitch on knitting needle.

2 Insert tapestry needle knitwise (as shown) through first stitch on back needle. Pull yarn through, leaving stitch on knitting needle.

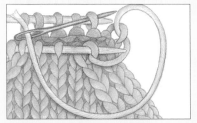

3 Insert tapestry needle knitwise through first stitch on front needle, slip stitch off needle and insert tapestry needle purlwise (as shown) through next stitch on front needle. Pull yarn through, leaving this stitch on needle.

4 Insert tapestry needle purlwise through first stitch on back needle. Slip stitch off needle and insert tapestry needle knitwise (as shown) through next stitch on back needle. Pull yarn through, leaving this stitch on needle.
Repeat steps 3 and 4 until all stitches on both front and back needles have been grafted. Fasten off and weave in end.

DUPLICATE STITCH

Duplicate stitch covers a knit stitch. Bring the needle up below the stitch to be worked. Insert the needle under both loops one row above and pull it through. Insert it back into the stitch below and through the center of the next stitch in one motion, as shown.

FINISHING

The pieces in this book use a variety of finishing techniques from crocheting around the edges to embroidery on the collar. Directions for making pompoms and tassels are on page 17. Also refer to the illustrations provided for other useful techniques: knitting with double-pointed needles, joining in the round, and Kitchener stitch.

HAND-SEWING

Several items in this book require hand-sewing in the finishing, such as the ribbon ties for the Bed Jacket on page 20, or the fur trim for the infant's jacket on page 74. Use a fine point hand sewing needle and sewing thread that matches the color of the trim. When sewing on ribbon, fold the end under and tack down with back stitch through all thicknesses. Cut the unsewn ends at an angle to prevent unraveling. When sewing on a trim, use back stitch and keep the stitches small and even.

CARE

Refer to the yarn label for the recommended cleaning method. Many of the projects in the book can be either washed by hand, or in the machine on a gentle or wool cycle, in lukewarm water with a mild detergent. Do not agitate, or soak for more than 10 minutes. Rinse gently with tepid water, then fold in a towel and gently press the water out. Lay flat to dry away from excess heat and light. Check the yarn band for any specific care instructions such as dry cleaning or tumble drying.

TO BEGIN SEAMING

If you have left a long tail from your cast-on row, you can use this strand to begin sewing. To make a neat join at the lower edge with no gap, use the technique shown here. Thread the strand into a yarn needle. With the rights sides of both pieces facing you, insert the yarn needle from back to front into the corner stitch of the piece without the tail. Making a figure eight with the yarn, insert the needle from back to front into the stitch with the cast-on tail. Tighten to close the gap.

INVISIBLE SEAMING: STOCKINETTE ST

To make an invisible side seam in a garment worked in stockinette stitch, insert the tapestry needle under the horizontal bar between the first and second stitches. Insert the needle into the corresponding bar on the other piece. Pull the yarn gently until the sides meet. Continue alternating from side to side.

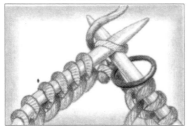

Hold the needle tip with the last cast-on stitch in your right hand and the tip with the first cast-on stitch in your left hand. Knit the first cast-on stitch, pulling the yarn tight to avoid a gap.

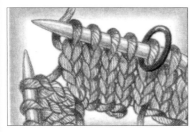

Work until you reach the marker. This completes the first round. Slip the marker to the right needle and work the next round.

TWISTED CORD

I If you have someone to help you, insert a pencil or knitting needle through each end of the strands. If not, place one end over a doorknob and put a pencil through the other end. Turn the strands clockwise until they are tightly twisted.

2 Keeping the strands taut, fold the piece in half. Remove the pencils and allow the cords to twist onto themselves.

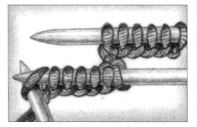

I Cast on the required number of stitches on the first needle, plus one extra. Slip this extra stitch to the next needle as shown. Continue in this way, casting on the required number of stitches on the last needle.

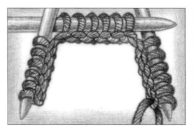

2 Arrange the needles as shown, with the cast-on edge facing the center of the triangle (or square).

3 Place a stitch marker after the last cast-on stitch. With the free needle, knit the first cast-on stitch, pulling the yarn tightly. Continue knitting in rounds, slipping the marker before beginning each round.

CHAIN

1 Pass the yarn over the hook and catch it with the hook.

2 Draw the yarn through the loop on the hook.

3 Repeat steps 1 and 2 to make a chain.

SINGLE CROCHET

1 Insert the hook through top two loops of a stitch. Pass the yarn over the hook and draw up a loop—two loops on hook.

2 Pass the yarn over the hook and draw through both loops on hook.

3 Continue in the same way, inserting the hook into each stitch.

HALF-DOUBLE CROCHET

1 Pass the yarn over the hook. Insert the hook through the top two loops of a stitch.

2 Pass the yarn over the hook and draw up a loop—three loops on hook. Pass the yarn over the hook.

3 Draw through all three loops on hook.

DOUBLE CROCHET

1 Pass the yarn over the hook. Insert the hook through the top two loops of a stitch.

2 Pass the yarn over the hook and draw up a loop— three loops on hook.

3 Pass the yarn over the hook and draw it through the first two loops on the hook, pass the yarn over the hook and draw through the remaining two loops. Continue in the same way, inserting the hook into each stitch.

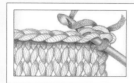

SLIP STITCH

Insert the crochet hook into a stitch, catch the yarn and pull up a loop. Draw the loop through the loop on the hook.

Illustrations: Joni Coniglio

POMPOM TEMPLATE

LAZY DAISY STITCH

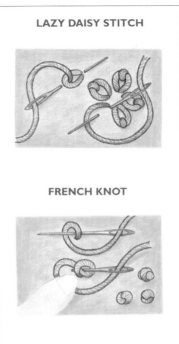

FRENCH KNOT

POMPOMS

1 Following the template, cut two circular pieces of cardboard.

2 Hold the two circles together and wrap the yarn tightly around the cardboard several times. Secure and carefully cut the yarn.

3 Tie a piece of yarn tightly between the two circles. Remove the cardboard and trim the pompom to the desired size.

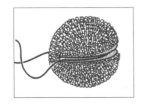

TASSELS

Cut a piece of card board to the desired length of the tassel. Wrap yarn around the cardboard. Knot a piece of yarn tightly around one end, cut as shown, and remove the cardboard. Wrap and tie yarn around the tassel about 1"/2.5cm down from the top to secure the fringe.

KNITTING TERMS AND ABBREVIATIONS

approx approximately

beg begin(ning)

bind off Used to finish an edge and keep stitches from unraveling. Lift the first stitch over the second, the second over the third, etc. (UK: cast off)

cast on A foundation row of stitches placed on the needle in order to begin knitting.

CC contrast color

ch chain(s)

cm centimeter(s)

cont continue(ing)

dc double crochet (UK: tr-treble)

dec decrease(ing)–Reduce the stitches in a row (knit 2 together).

dpn double-pointed needle(s)

foll follow(s)(ing)

g gram(s)

garter stitch Knit every row. Circular knitting: knit one round, then purl one round.

hdc half double crochet (UK: htr-half treble)

inc increase(ing)–Add stitches in a row (knit into the front and back of a stitch).

k knit

k2tog knit 2 stitches together

LH left-hand

lp(s) loop(s)

m meter(s)

M1 make one stitch–With the needle tip, lift the strand between last stitch worked and next stitch on the left-hand needle and knit into the back of it. One stitch has been added.

YARN SYMBOLS

① **Fine Weight**
(29-32 stitches per 4"/10cm)
Includes baby and fingering yarns, and some of the heavier crochet cottons. The range of needle sizes is 0-4 (2-3.5mm).

② **Lightweight**
(25-28 stitches per 4"/10cm)
Includes sport yarn, sock yarn, UK 4-ply, and lightweight DK yarns. The range of needle sizes is 3-6 (3.25-4mm).

③ **Medium Weight**
(21-24 stitches per 4"/10cm)
Includes DK and worsted, the most commonly used knitting yarns. The range of needle sizes is 6-9 (4-5.5mm).

④ **Medium-heavy Weight**
(17-20 stitches per 4"/10cm)
Also called heavy worsted or Aran. The range of needle sizes is 8-10 (5-6mm).

⑤ **Bulky Weight**
(13-16 stitches per 4"/10cm)
Also called chunky. Includes heavier Icelandic yarns. The range of needle sizes is 10-11 (6-8mm).

⑥ **Extra-bulky Weight**
(9-12 stitches per 4"/10cm)
The heaviest yarns available. The range of needle sizes is 11 and up (8mm and up).

MC main color

mm millimeter(s)

no stitch On some charts, "no stitch" is indicated with shaded spaces where stitches have been decreased or not yet made. In such cases, work the stitches of the chart, skipping over the "no stitch" spaces.

oz ounce(s)

p purl

p2tog purl 2 stitches together

pat(s) pattern

pick up and knit (purl) Knit (or purl) into the loops along an edge.

pm place markers–Place or attach a loop of contrast yarn or purchased stitch marker as indicated.

psso pass slip stitch(es) over

rem remain(s)(ing)

rep repeat

rev St st reverse Stockinette stitch–Purl right-side rows, knit wrong-side rows. Circular knitting: purl all rounds. (UK: reverse stocking stitch)

rnd(s) round(s)

RH right-hand

RS right side(s)

sc single crochet (UK: dc-double crochet)

sk skip

SKP Slip 1, knit 1, pass slip stitch over knit 1.

SK2P Slip 1, knit 2 together, pass slip stitch over the knit 2 together.

sl slip–An unworked stitch made by passing a stitch from the left-hand to the right-hand needle as if to purl.

sl st slip stitch (UK: single crochet)

ssk slip, slip, knit–Slip next 2 stitches knitwise, one at a time, to right-hand needle. Insert tip of left-hand needle into fronts of these stitches from left to right. Knit them together. One stitch has been decreased.

sssk Slip next 3 sts knitwise, one at a time, to right-hand needle. Insert tip of left-hand needle into fronts of these stitches from left to right. Knit them together. Two stitches have been decreased.

st(s) stitch(es)

St st Stockinette stitch–Knit right-side rows, purl wrong-side rows. Circular knitting: knit all rounds. (UK: stocking stitch)

tbl through back of loop

tog together

WS wrong side(s)

wyib with yarn in back

wyif with yarn in front

work even Continue in pattern without increasing or decreasing. (UK: work straight)

yd yard(s)

yo yarn over–Make a new stitch by wrapping the yarn over the right-hand needle. (UK: yfwd, yon, yrn)

* = repeat directions following * as many times as indicated.

[ ] = Repeat directions inside brackets as many times as indicated.

BED JACKET
Bed & breakfast

Sentimental moments. When confined to bed, women of the 1940s were never without this bedroom basic. Knit in luxurious cashmere and a dainty mock-cable rib.

SIZE
■ One size.

KNITTED MEASUREMENTS
■ Bust 42"/106cm
■ Length 20½"/52cm
■ Upper arm 13¼"/33.5cm

MATERIALS
■ .88oz/25g balls (each approx 120yd/110m) of Grignasco/JCA *Cashmere* (cashmere ③) in #406 blue
■ One pair each sizes 2 and 6 (2.5 and 4mm) needles *or size to obtain gauge*
■ Size C/2 (2.5mm) crochet hook
■ ¾yd/20m of ¼"/6mm ribbon

GAUGES
■ 28 sts and 32 rows to 4"/10cm over body pat st using larger needles.
■ 28 sts and 38 rows to 4"/10cm over yoke pat st using smaller needles.
Take time to check gauges.

BODY PATTERN STITCH
(multiple of 6 sts plus 3)
Row 1 (RS) *P3, k3; rep from*, end p3.
Row 2 *K3, p3; rep from *, end k3.
Row 3 *P3, sl 1 knitwise, k2, pass sl st over the two k sts; rep from *, end p3.
Row 4 *K3, p1, yo, p1; rep from *, end k3.
Rep rows 1-4 rows for body pat st.

BACK
With larger needles, cast on 147 sts.
Work in body pat st until piece measures 12"/30.5cm from beg, end with row 4.

Armhole shaping
Bind off 6 sts at beg of next 2 rows. Dec 1 st each side every other row 6 times—123 sts. Work pat row 3—103 sts. Change to smaller needles.

Yoke pattern
Row 1 (WS) K1, p1, k1, *p2, k1, p1, k1; rep from * to end.
Row 2 P1, k1, p1, *k2, p1, k1, p1; rep from * to end.
Row 3 Rep row 1.
Row 4 P1, k1, p1, *insert needle in back of 2nd st on LH needle and k this st, do not drop st from needle, k first st, drop both sts from LH needle, p1, k1, p1; rep from * to end.
Rep these 4 rows for yoke pat until armhole measures 7"/18cm.

Shoulder shaping
Bind off 8 sts at beg of next 2 rows, 5 sts at the beg of next 10 rows. Bind off 37 sts for back neck.

RIGHT FRONT
With larger needles, cast on 75 sts. Work in body pat for 12"/30.5cm, end at armhole edge with pat row 1. Shape armhole as for back—63 sts. Work pat row 3—53 sts. Change to smaller needles and work yoke pat as for back until armhole measures 5¼"/13cm, end at front edge with pat row 4.

Neck and shoulder shaping
Bind off 10 sts for neck. Dec 1 st at neck edge every other row 10 times, AT SAME TIME, work shoulder shaping as for back when armhole measures 7"/18cm.

LEFT FRONT

Work to correspond to right front, reversing all shaping.

SLEEVES

With larger needles, cast on 141 sts. Work body pat st for 3"/7.5cm, end with pat row 1.

Dec row (WS) K3, [p3tog] 3 times, *k3, p3, k3, [p3tog] 3 times; rep from * 6 times more, end k3—93 sts.

Next row Work pat row 3. Cont pat until piece measures 9"/23cm from beg.

Cap shaping

Work as for back armhole shaping—69 sts. Work even until cap measures 4½"/11.5cm. Dec 1 st each side of next row, then every other row twice more. Bind off 3 sts at beg of next 8 rows. Bind off rem 39 sts.

FINISHING

Block pieces to measurements. Sew shoulder seams. Set in sleeves, taking a 2½"/6.5cm box pleat at top center to ease in extra fullness. Sew side and sleeve seams. With crochet hook, work an edge of sc around center fronts and neck edges, working 3 sc in each top corner. Cut two 18"/45.5cm lengths of ribbon. Sew ribbon to WS of jacket fronts at top, sewing down for 1"/2.5cm to secure.

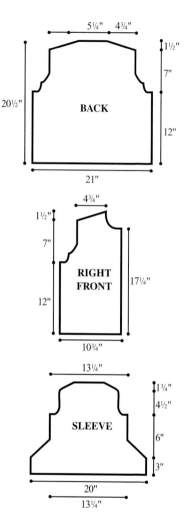

MAN'S SOCKS
Chevron classic

Hand-made socks were a 1950s staple, always knit in a fine, durable wool/nylon sock yarn. This four-needle style features subtle purl-stitch chevrons and traditional patterning.

SIZE

Instructions are written for man's size Medium (10½-11½).

MATERIALS

▨ 2 1¾oz/50g balls (each approx 222yd/205m) of Stahl Wolle/Tahki•Stacy Charles, Inc. *Socka* 50 (wool ①) in #9422 green/blue
▨ One set (4) size 1 (2.25mm) dpn *or size to obtain gauge*
▨ Stitch markers

GAUGE

36 sts and 42 rnds/rows to 4"/10cm over St st using size 1 (2.25mm) needles.
Take time to check gauge.

CUFF

Beg at top edge, cast on 68 sts. Divide sts evenly over three needles. Join, taking care not to twist sts on needles. Mark end of rnd and sl marker every rnd. Work in k2, p2 rib for 3"/7.5cm, inc 4 sts evenly spaced on last rnd—72 sts.

Beg pat st

Rnd 1 Work pat st foll chart row 1, working 24-st rep 3 times. Cont to foll chart in this way through rnd 32. Work rnds 1-32 once, then rep rnds 1-14 once more. Piece measures approx 10"/25.5cm from beg.

HEEL

Next rnd Work 54 sts, work last 18 sts and sl these sts plus first 18 sts to one needle to work for heel, sl rem 36 sts to two needles on hold for instep. Work back and forth on 36 heel sts only as foll:

Row 1 (WS) Sl 1 purlwise, p to end.
Row 2 (RS) *Sl 1 purlwise, k1; rep from * to end.
Rep these 2 rows 17 times more (for 36 rows).

Turn heel

Next row (WS) Sl 1, p20, p2tog, p1, turn.
Row 2 Sl 1, k7, SKP, k1, turn.
Row 3 Sl 1, p8, p2tog, p1, turn.
Row 4 Sl 1, k9, SKP, k1, turn.
Cont to work in this way always having 1 more st before dec, and work SKP on RS rows or p2tog on WS rows, until there are 22 sts on heel needle.

GUSSETS AND FOOT

With same needle, pick up and k18 sts along side edge of heel, work 36 instep sts on 1 needle (cont with pat), with free needle, pick up and k 18 sts along other side edge of heel, k first 11 sts of heel needle onto last needle—29 sts on *Needle 1* and *Needle 3*, 36 sts on *Needle 2*, for a total of 94 sts. Mark center of sole as end of rnd. Cont in pat st on instep sts and St st on rem sts for 1 rnd.

Next rnd K to last 3 sts of *Needle 1*, k2tog, k1; work even over *Needle 2* (instep sts), on needle 3, k1, SKP, k to end. Rep last 2 rnds 10 time more—72 sts. Work even through 4th rep of 32-row chart pat st. Discontinue chart and cont in St st on all sts until foot measures 8½"/21.5cm or 2"/5cm less than desired length from back of heel to end of toe. Make adjustments in length at this point.

Shape toe

Beg at center of sole, k to last 3 sts of *Needle 1*, k2tog, k1; on *Needle 2*, k1, SKP, k to last 3 sts of *Needle 2*, k2tog, k1, on *Needle 3*, k1, SKP, k to end. K 1 rnd. Rep last 2 rnds 12 times more—20 sts. Sl first 5 sts of *Needle 1* to *Needle 3*. Hold 2 needles tog and parallel. Weave sts tog using Kitchener st.

FINISHING

Block socks lightly.

Stitch Key

■ K on RS, p on WS

⊟ P on RS, k on WS

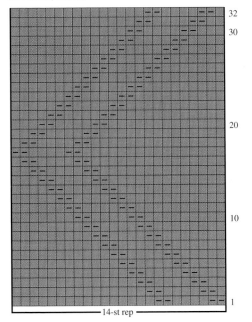

14-st rep

RIBBED AND CABLED SCARF
Enduring classic

Fine alpaca yarn brings extra warmth to this 1940s winter wardrobe staple. Classic rib and cable patterning is easy to knit, yet it remains strikingly handsome.

KNITTED MEASUREMENTS
■ Approx 9" x 45½"/23cm x 116cm

MATERIALS
■ 6 1¾oz/50g hanks (each approx 116yd/105m) of Classic Elite Yarns *Inca Alpaca* (alpaca ③) in #1155 red heather
■ One pair size 5 (3.75mm) needles *or size to obtain gauge*
■ Cable needle

GAUGE
30 sts and 28 rows to 4"/10cm over k1, p1 rib using size 5 (3.75mm) needles.
Take time to check gauge.

STITCH GLOSSARY
6-st RC
Sl 3 sts to cn and hold to *back*, k3, k3 from cn.

CABLE AND RIB PATTERN
Rows 1, 3 and 7 (RS) [K1, p1] 7 times, k1, *p2, k6, p2, k1, p2, k6, p2, [k1, p1] 7 times, k1; rep from * once.
Row 2 and all WS rows [P1, k1] 7 times, p1, *k2, p6, k2, p1, k2, p6, k2, [p1, k1] 7 times, p1; rep from *once.
Row 5 [K1, p1] 7 times, k1, *p2, 6-st RC, p2, k1, p2, 6-st RC, p2, [k1, p1] 7 times, k1; rep from * once.
Row 8 Rep row 2.
Rep rows 1-8 for cable and rib pat.

SCARF
Cast on 87 sts. Work in cable and rib pat until piece measures 45½"/116cm from beg. Bind off.

FINISHING
Block to measurements.

Early bloomer

A snug-fitting bodice accented with balloon-style pants was the fashion silhouette for postwar newborns. From the 1940s, this romper has become a classic.

SIZES

■ Instructions are written for size 6 months. Changes for size 12 months are in parentheses.

KNITTED MEASUREMENTS

■ Chest 17 (18½)"/43 (47)cm
■ Length 15 (16½)"/38 (42)cm
■ Upperarm 5¾ (6½)"/14.5 (16.5)cm

MATERIALS

■ 2 (3) 1¾oz/50g balls (each approx 222yd/203m) of Brown Sheep Co. *Cotton Fine* (cotton/wool ①) in #CF690 lilac
■ One pair each sizes 1 and 2 (2.25 and 2.5mm) needles *or size to obtain gauge*
■ Size 5 (1.75mm) steel crochet hook
■ Three ½"/13mm buttons
■ 2 snap fasteners
■ Stitch holders

GAUGE

36 sts and 44 rows to 4"/10cm over St st using larger needles.
Take time to check gauge.

YOKE PATTERN STITCH

(multiple of 6 sts plus 4)
Row 1 (RS) *P4, k2; rep from *, end p4.
Row 2 *K4, p2; rep from *, end k4.

Row 3 *K2, p4; rep from *, end k2, p2.
Row 4 K2, *p2, k4; rep from *, end p2.
Rep rows 1-4 for yoke pat st.

BACK

With larger needles, cast on 18 sts. Work in k1, p1 rib for 4 rows. Cast on 11 (10) sts at beg of next 12 (14) rows—150 (158) sts. Cont in St st until piece measures 8 (9)"/20.5 (23)cm from beg, end with a WS row.
Next row (RS) K1 (3), *k2tog; rep from *, end k1 (3)—76 (82) sts. Change to smaller needles and work in k1, p1 rib for 1"/2.5cm. Change to larger needles and cont in St st until piece measures 3 (3½)"/7.5 (9)cm above rib.

Armhole shaping
Bind off 3 sts at beg of next 2 rows—70 (76) sts. Work even until armhole measures 1¼ (1¾)"/3 (4.5)cm, end with a WS row.

YOKE

Change to yoke pat st and work even until armhole measures 2¾ (3¼)"/7 (8)cm
Neck shaping
Next row (RS) Work 21 (24) sts, sl center 28 sts on holder, join 2nd ball of yarn and work to end. Working both sides at once, dec 1 st from each neck edge every other row 3 times—18 (21) sts rem each side. Work even until armhole measures 3¼ (3½)"/8 (9)cm.
Shoulder shaping
Bind off 6 (7) sts from each armhole edge 3 times.

FRONT

Work as for back until armhole measures ¾ (1)"/2 (2.5)cm, end with a WS row.

YOKE

Row I (RS) K18, work yoke pat st on center 34 (40) sts, k rem 18 sts.

Cont to work center 34 (40) sts in yoke pat st and 18 sts each side in St st until 6 rows of pat have been completed. Change to yoke pat st across all 70 (76) sts. Work even until armhole measures 2¼ (2½)"/6 (6.5)cm.

Neck and shoulder shaping

Work as for back neck and shoulder shaping.

SLEEVES

With smaller needles, cast on 36 (44) sts. Work in k1, p1 rib for 6 rows. P next row, inc 16 sts evenly spaced—52 (60) sts. Change to larger needles and cont in St st until piece measures 2 (2½)"/5 (6.5)cm from beg.

Cap shaping

Bind off 3 sts at beg of next 2 rows. Dec 1 st each side every other row 11 (14) times. Bind off 3 sts at beg of next 4 rows. Bind off rem 12 (14) sts.

FINISHING

Block pieces to measurements. Sew right shoulder seam. Seam left shoulder for 1"/2.5cm from armhole edge. Sew side and sleeve seams. Set in sleeves.

Neckband

With RS facing and smaller needles, pick up and k 91 sts around neck, including sts from holders. Work in k1, p1 rib for ¾"/2cm. Bind off in rib With crochet hook, work 2 rows sc on left shoulder opening, making three ch-4 button loops evenly spaced on front.

Legbands

With smaller needles, pick up and k 132 (140) sts around one leg. P next row, dec 52 sts evenly spaced—80 (88) sts. Work in k1, p1 rib for 4 rows. Bind off in rib. Work other leg to correspond. Close crotch with snap fasteners. Sew 3 buttons on left back shoulder to correspond to button loops.

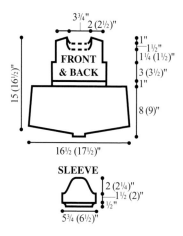

MAN'S V-NECK VEST

Racing stripes

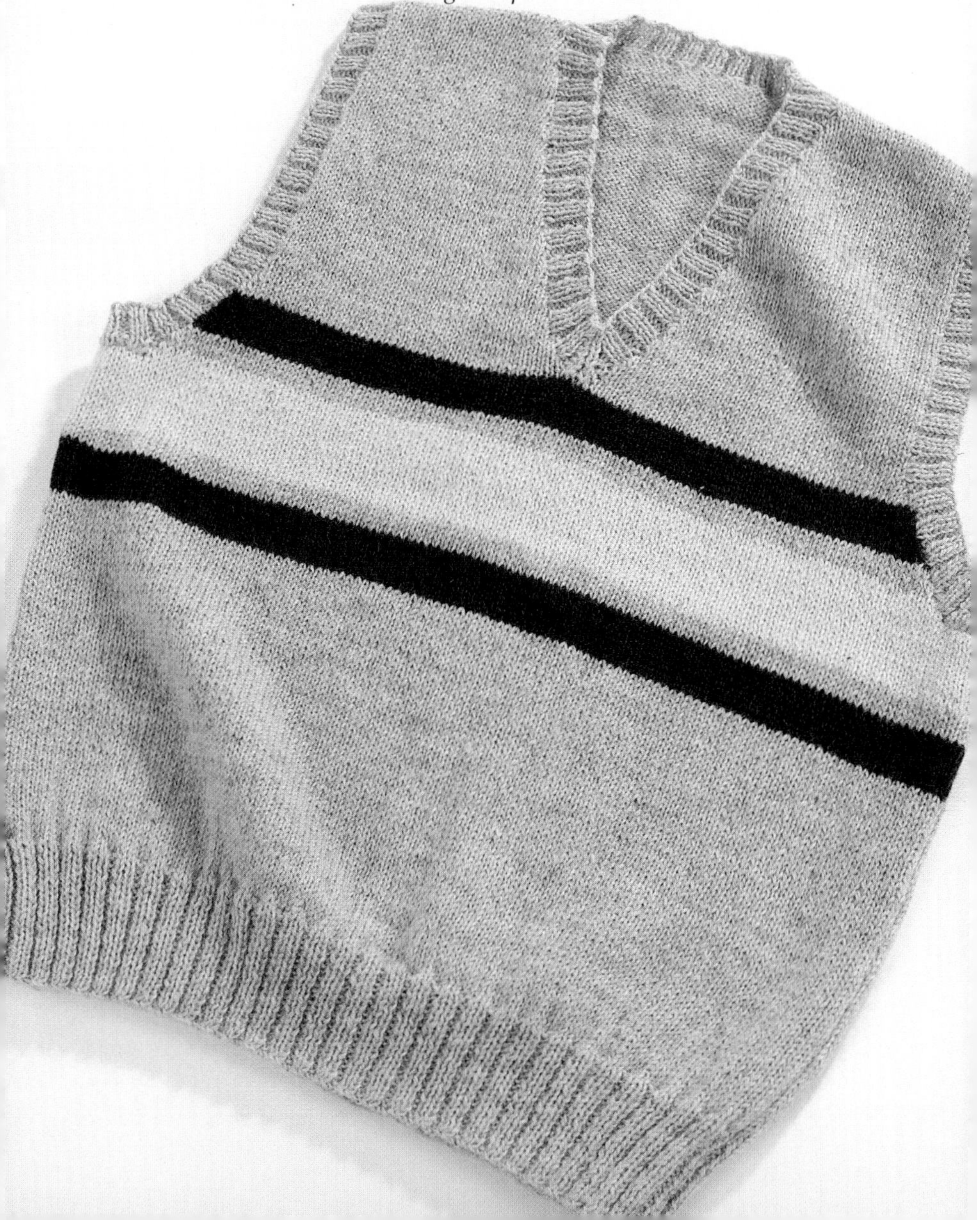

This vest's sporty striping creates a casual modern look for discerning men of all ages. Fitted, V-neck styling was a '50s staple for the well-dressed man.

SIZES

Instructions are written for Man's size Small. Changes for sizes Medium and Large are in parentheses.

KNITTED MEASUREMENTS

- Chest 40 (42, 44)"/101.5 (106.5, 111.5)cm
- Length 23¼ (24¼, 24¾)"/59 (61.5, 63)cm

MATERIALS

- 2 (3, 3) 8¾oz/250g balls (each approx 525yd/435m) of Wool Pak Yarn NZ/Baabajoes Wool Co. Yarn *8 Ply* (wool ③) in mist (MC)
- 1 hank each in dk green (A) and natural (B)
- One pair each sizes 2 and 4 (2.5 and 3.5mm) needles *or size to obtain gauge*
- One set (5) size 2 (2.5mm) dpn
- Stitch holder

GAUGE

23 sts and 30 rows to 4"/10cm over St st using larger needles.
Take time to check gauge.

STRIPE PATTERN

Work 8 rows A, 4 rows MC, 16 rows B, 4 rows MC, and 8 rows A.

BACK

With smaller needles and MC, cast on 114 (120, 126) sts. Work in k2, p2 rib for 3"/7.5cm. Change to larger needles and cont in St st until piece measures 9½ (10, 10½)"/24 (25.5, 27)cm from beg. Work striped pat, AT SAME TIME, when piece measures 12½ (13, 13½)"/32 (33, 34)cm from beg, work armhole shaping as foll:

Armhole shaping

Bind off 8 sts at beg of next 2 rows. Dec 1 st each side every other row 9 (10, 11) times—80 (84, 88) sts. When stripe pat is completed, cont with MC only and work even until armholes measures 10 (10½, 10½)"/25.5 (26.5, 26.5)cm.

Shoulder shaping

Bind off 7 (8, 9) sts at beg of next 4 rows, 8 sts at beg of next 2 rows. Sl rem 36 sts to a holder for back neck.

FRONT

Work as for back until armhole measures 2½"/6.5cm and stripe pat is complete.

Neck shaping

Next row (RS) Cont armhole shaping, k to center, join a 2nd ball of yarn and work to end. Cont to work both sides at once, dec 1 st at each neck edge on next RS row, then every other row 4 times more, every 4th row 13 times—22 (24, 26) sts rem each side. Work even until same length as back to shoulders.

Shoulder shaping

Bind off 7 (8, 9) sts from each shoulder edge twice, 8 sts once.

FINISHING

Block pieces to measurements. Sew shoulder and side seams.

Neckband

With MC and dpn, pick up and k 136 (144, 144) sts around V-neck, including sts from holder. Join and work in k2, p2 rib, keeping 2 sts at point of V as k2. Dec 1 st each side of these k2 sts every other row for 1"/2.5cm. Bind off loosely in rib.

6¼" 3¾ (4, 4½)"

¾"

8¼ (8¾, 8¾)"

15 (15½, 16)"

9½ (10, 10½)" 10 (10½, 10½)"

FRONT & BACK

3"

20 (21, 22)"

Two easy pieces are joined together to create this '50s "shoulderette." Perfect for throwing on over a party frock in the cool of evening, or to wear while relaxing at home, it can also double as a bed jacket.

SIZES
■ One size

KNITTED MEASUREMENTS
■ Center back neck to cuff 14"/35.5cm
■ Length 19½"/49.5cm

MATERIALS
■ 6 1¾oz/50g balls (each approx 202yd/184m) of Jaeger Handknits *Alpaca* (alpaca ②) in #384 peach
■ One pair size 3 (3mm) needles *or size to obtain gauge*
■ Size 3 (3mm) circular needle, 36"/92cm long
■ Size C/2 (2.5mm) crochet hook

GAUGE
28 sts and 50 rows to 4"/10cm over pat st

using size 3 (3mm) needles.
Take time to check gauge.

Note Cast on and beg with circular needle, then change to straight needles when there are fewer sts.

PATTERN STITCH
Rows 1 and 3 (RS) Knit.
Rows 2 and 5 Purl.
Rows 4 and 6 Knit.
Rep rows 1-6 for pat st.

SHOULDERETTE
(make 2 pieces)
Cast on 269 sts for inside edge of one half. Work in pat st for 8 rows.
Next row K22, pm, *k45, pm; rep from * 4 times more, k22.
Dec row Dec 1 st each side of each marker—257 sts. Rep dec row every 12th row 13 times more, having 1 st less before first marker and 1 st less after last marker and 2 sts less between markers after each dec row—101 sts. Work even for 7 rows.
Next row K1, *k2tog, k2; rep from * to

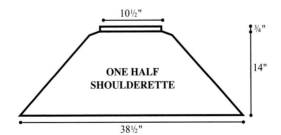

10½"

¾"

ONE HALF
SHOULDERETTE

14"

38½"

end—76 sts. Work in k2, p2 rib for ¾"/2cm for cuff. Bind off in rib. Make 2nd piece in same way.

FINISHING

Block pieces. Fold each piece in half and sew each piece tog along sides of rows from cast-on to bound-off cuff edge. Mark center of cast-on edge of each piece for shoulder. Beg 3"/7.5cm below shoulder markers, sew the pieces tog for 10"/25.5cm for center back, leaving rem sts free. With crochet hook, work 1 row sc around free edges keeping work flat.

PLAID SLIPPERS
Sole mates

Knitting for the heart and sole, these classic 1940s drawstring slippers are worked in a striking two-color plaid design. Purchased suede soles are sewn to crocheted base soles, which are deeper at the heel than at the toe for added comfort and warmth.

KNITTED MEASUREMENTS

■ Instructions are for size 4-5. Changes for size 6-7 and size 8-9 are in parentheses.

MATERIALS

■ 4 1¾oz/50g balls (each approx 115yd/104m) of Naturally/S.R. Kertzer *Luxury DK* (wool/mohair ③) in #914 red (MC)

■ 2 balls in #923 white (CC)

■ One pair size 1 (2.25mm) needles *or size to obtain gauge*

■ 1 pair "Suede Slipper Soles" from Fiber Trends (304 36th St #173, Bellingham, WA 98225)

■ Sizes 2 steel and E/4 (3.5mm) crochet hooks

■ 1yd/1m Offray double faced satin ribbon ⅛"/3mm wide

GAUGE

28 sts and 34 rows = 4"/10cm over pat st using size 1 (2.25mm) needles.
Take time to check gauge.

STRIPE PATTERN

*6 rows of MC, 2 rows of CC, 2 rows of MC, 1 row CC; rep from *11 rows) for stripe pat.

Note

Vertical stripes are worked with CC in a chain st with crochet hook into the purl ridges after pieces are knit.

LOWER SOLE

With a double strand of MC and larger crochet hook, ch 35 (37, 39)—7½ (8, 8½)"/19 (20.5, 21.5)cm

Rnd 1 Work 3 sc in 2nd ch from hook, sc in next 32 (34, 36) ch, 3 sc in last ch, working across opposite side of foundation ch, sc in next 32 (34, 36) ch.

Rnd 2 Work 2 sc in next 3 sc, sc in next 15 (16, 17) sc, hdc in next 7 sc, dc in next 8 (9, 10) sc, hdc in next 2 sc, 2 sc in next 3 sc, hdc in next 2 sc, dc in next 8 (9,10) sc, hdc in next 7 sc, sc in next 15 (16, 17) sc.

Rnd 3 Work 2 sc in next 6 sc, sc in next 15 (16, 17) sc, hdc in next 7 hdc, dc in next 8 (9, 10) dc, hdc in next 2 hdc, 2 sc in next 6 sc, hdc in next 2 hdc, dc in next 8 (9, 10) dc, hdc in next 7 hdc, sc in next 15 (16, 17) sc.

Rnd 4 Work [2 sc in next sc, sc in next sc] 6 times, sc in next 15 (16, 17) sc, hdc in next 7 hdc, dc in next 8 (9, 10) dc, hdc in next 2 hdc, sc in next 12 sc, hdc in next 2 hdc, dc in next 8 (9, 10) dc, hdc in next 7 hdc, sc in next 15 (16, 17) sc, sl st in next 2 sc. Cut yarn.

UPPER SOLE

Work as for lower sole for 3rd rnds. Cut

MC and attach a double strand of CC. Complete as for lower sole.

LOWER HEEL WEDGE

With a double strand of MC and larger crochet hook, ch 17 (18, 19) sts.

Row 1 Sc in 2nd ch from hook, sc in next 15 (16, 17) ch, 3 sc in last ch, working back across opposite side of foundation ch, sc in next 15 (16, 17) ch, ch 1, turn.

Row 2 Sc in next 15 (16, 17) sc, 2 sc in next 3 sc, sc in next 15 (16, 17) sc, ch 1, turn.

Row 3 Sc in next 15 (16, 17) sc, 2 sc in next 6 sc, sc in next 15 (16, 17) sc. Cut MC, attach a double strand of CC. Ch 1, turn.

Row 4 Sc in next 15 (16-17) sc, [2 sc in next sc, sc in next sc] 6 times, sc in next 15 (16, 17) sc. Break yarn.

UPPER HEEL WEDGE

With a double strand of MC and larger crochet hook, ch 11 (12, 13) sts.

Row 1 Sc in 2nd ch from hook, sc in next 9 (10, 11) ch, 3 sc in last ch, working along opposite side of starting ch, sc in next 9 (10, 11) ch, ch 1, turn.

Row 2 Sc in next 9 (10, 11) sc, 2 sc in next 3 sc, sc in next 9 (10, 11) sc, ch 1, turn.

Row 3 Sc in next 9 (10, 11) sc, 2 sc in next 6 sc, sc in next 9 (10, 11) sc, ch 1, turn.

Row 4 Sc in next 9 (10, 11) sc, [2 sc in next sc, sc in next sc] 6 times, sc in next 9 (10, 11) sc. Break yarn.

RIGHT SIDE

Beg at back edge with a single strand of MC and size 1 (2.25mm) needles, cast on 29 (31, 33) sts tightly.

Row 1 K3 (4, 5), [p2, k2, p1, k4] twice, p2, k2, p1, k3 (4, 5).

Row 2 P3 (4, 5), [k1, p2, k2, p4] twice, k1, p2. k2, p3 (4, 5).

Rep these 2 rows for pat, and work in stripe pat for 4½ (5, 5½)"/11 (12.5, 14)cm, end with a k row. Cont in pat as established, dec 2 sts at beg of next row as foll: sl 1, p2tog, psso. Dec 2 sts at same edge each row until 19 (21, 23) sts rem, then dec 1 st every other row until 9 (11, 12) sts rem. *Work even for 3 (5, 7) rows, dec 1 st at top edge next row. Rep from * once more. Dec 1 st at top edge each row until 4 (5, 6) sts rem. Bind off.

LEFT SIDE

Beg at back edge with single strand of MC, cast on 29 (31, 33) sts.

Row 1 K3 (4, 5), [p1, k2, p2 k4] twice, p1, k2, p2, k3 (4, 5).

Row 2 P3 (4, 5), [k2, p2, k1, p4] twice, k2, p2, k1, p3 (4, 5). Rep rows 1 and 2 for reversed pat. Complete to correspond with right side.

PLAID

With RS facing, CC and smaller crochet hook, attach yam in a p st at cast-on edge. Holding loose end of yarn underneath work. *Insert hook through center of next p st and pull up a lp, draw lp through lp on hook. Rep from * along p rib. Work chain st in this way through each p-st rib, keeping ch sts same size as k-sts.

FINISHING

Block pieces. Sew front seam, matching plaid. Press seam open. Place lower sole, RS down, with purchased sole on top. Pin lower heel wedge and upper heel wedge in place, then upper sole, right side up. With a single strand of MC, sew crocheted pieces tog, concealing purchased sole, working through all thicknesses. Sew shoe to sole. Sew down top edge of slipper to WS to form casing. Run ribbon through casing and tie at center back.

A fireside look popular in the late 1950s, this relaxed pullover looks new again with its cropped, body-skimming shape, two-piece portrait collar and 3/4-sleeve styling. The deeper back adds to the glamour of the era.

SIZES

Instructions are written for size Small. Changes for sizes Medium and Large are in parentheses.

KNITTED MEASUREMENTS

- Bust 39½ (42, 44)"/100 (106.5, 111.5)cm
- Length 18¼ (18½, 18¾)"/46.5 (47, 47.5)cm
- Upper arm 14 (14½, 15)"/35.5 (37, 38)cm

MATERIALS

- 9 (10, 11) 1¾oz/50g balls (each approx 88yd/80m) of Tahki•Stacy Charles, Inc. *Luna* (wool ⑤) in #218 purple
- One pair size 10½ (6.5mm) needles *or size to obtain gauge*
- Stitch markers

GAUGE

14 sts and 20 rows to 4"/10cm over St st using size 10½ (6.5mm) needles.
Take time to check gauge.
Note Back and front have a different number of sts up to the armhole. The schematic reflects ½ the bust measurement.

BACK

Cast on 67 (71, 75) sts.
Row 1 (RS) K1, *p1, k1; rep from * to end. Rep this row for seed st until 8 rows are worked from beg. Then cont in St st until piece measures 10½"/26.5cm from beg.

Armhole shaping

Bind off 3 sts at beg of next 2 rows. Dec 1 st each side every other row 5 (6, 7) times—51 (53, 55) sts. Work even until armhole measures 4¼ (4½, 4¾)"/11 (11.5, 12)cm.

DIVIDE FOR NECK

Next row (RS) K18 (19, 20), join 2nd ball of yarn and bind off center 15 sts, k to end. Working both sides at once, dec 1 st at each neck edge *every* row 6 times, every other row 3 times—9 (10, 11) sts rem each side.

Shoulder shaping

Bind off 3 sts from each shoulder edge twice, 3 (4, 5) sts once.

FRONT

Cast on 71 (75, 79) sts. Work as for back to armhole.

Armhole shaping

Bind off 5 sts at beg of next 2 rows. Dec 1 st each side every other row 5 (6, 7) times—51 (53, 55) sts. Complete as for back.

SLEEVES

Cast on 41 (43, 45) sts. Work seed st border as for back. Then cont in St st for 2 rows. Inc 1 st each side of next row, then every 12th row 3 times more—49 (51, 53) sts. Work even until piece measures 12"/30.5cm from beg.

Cap shaping

Bind off 4 sts at beg of next 2 rows. Dec 1 st each side every other row 5 times, every 4th row twice, then every other row 2 (3, 4) times. Bind off 2 sts at beg of next 4 rows. Bind off rem 15 sts.

Cast on 61 sts. Work 8 rows seed st border as for back.

Row 1 (RS) Work 5 sts in seed st, pm, k51, pm, work 5 sts in seed st.

Row 2 Work seed st to marker, p to 2nd marker, work 5 sts in seed st.

Rep these 2 rows until collar measures 5"/12.5cm.

Dec row Work to marker, k2tog, k2, k2tog, *k3, k2tog; rep from * to marker, work last 5 sts—50 sts. Bind off. Work 2nd half of collar in same way.

FINISHING

Block pieces to measurements. Sew shoulder, side and sleeve seams. Sew in sleeves. Sew both halves of collar to neck edge with edges of collar placed at center front and center back.

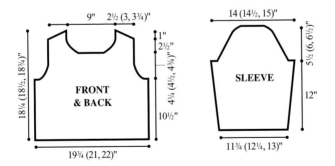

CARDIGAN WITH EMBROIDERED COLLAR

Rhapsody in bloom

For Intermediate Knitters

Hand-worked embroidery was the embellishment of choice during the '60s. Echoing the sweetness of Hungarian hand-work, a pretty collar of blossoming flowers accent this lovely child's cardigan.

SIZES

Instructions are written for Child's size 2. Changes for sizes 4 and 6 are in parentheses.

KNITTED MEASUREMENTS

- Chest 23½ (25, 27)"/59.5 (63.5, 68.5)cm
- Length 15¼ (16½, 18)"/39 (42, 45.5)cm
- Upper arm 9¼ (9½, 10½)"/23.5 (24, 26.5)cm

MATERIALS

- 13 (14, 15) .88/25g balls (each approx 92yd/85m) of Baruffa/Lane Borgosesia *Cash Silk* (wool/silk/cashmere ③) in #506 peach
- One pair each sizes 3 and 5 (3 and 3.75mm) needles *or size to obtain gauge*
- Size F/5 (4mm) crochet hook
- Six ⅝"/15mm buttons
- One snap fastener
- Embroidery Floss in coral, blue, gold and leaf green
- Tissue tracing paper (for embroidery)

GAUGE

20 sts and 32 rows to 4"/10cm over St st using larger needles.
Take time to check gauge.

BACK

With smaller needles, cast on 56 (60, 64) sts. Work in k1, p1 rib for 2"/5cm. Change to larger needles and work in St st until piece measures 9½ (10½, 11½)"/24 (27, 29)cm from beg.

Raglan armhole shaping

Bind off 2 sts at beg of next 2 rows. Dec 1 st each side every other row 18 (19, 21) times. Bind off rem 16 (18, 18) sts.

LEFT FRONT

With smaller needles, cast on 36 (38, 40) sts. Work in k1, p1 rib for 2"/5cm. Change to larger needles and cont in St st until piece measures 9½ (10½, 11½)"/24 (27, 29)cm from beg.

Raglan armhole shaping

Next row (RS) Bind off 2 sts, k to end. Cont to dec 1 st at armhole edge every other row 14 (15, 16) times.

Neck shaping

Next row (WS) Bind off 11 sts, work to end. Cont to dec 1 st at neck edge every other row 4 (4, 5) times, AT SAME TIME, dec 1 st at raglan armhole edge every other row 4 (5, 5) times more. Fasten off last st. Mark place for buttonholes, the first one ¾"/2cm from lower edge and the last one 1"/2.5cm below neck shaping and the others evenly spaced between.

RIGHT FRONT

Work to correspond to left front, reversing shaping and forming buttonholes opposite markers as foll:

Row I (RS) K2, bind off 3 sts, k to end.
Row 2 Purl, casting on 3 sts over the bound-off sts.

SLEEVES

With smaller needles, cast on 28 (30, 32) sts. Work in k1, p1 ribbing for 2"/5cm. Change to larger needles and work in St st, inc 1 st each side every 6th row 9 (9, 10) times—46 (48, 52) sts. Work even until piece measures 9 (10½, 11½)"/23 (26.5, 29)cm from beg.
Raglan cap shaping
Bind off 2 sts at beg of next 2 rows. Dec 1 st each side every other row 18 (19, 21) times. Bind off rem 6 sts.

FINISHING

Block pieces to measurements. Sew raglan sleeves into armholes. Sew side and sleeve seams.

COLLAR

With larger needles and working from WS of garment, pick up and k 66 (70, 72) sts evenly around neck edge, beg and end at center of 11-st bind off on fronts. Work in St st (beg with a p row) for 3"/7.5cm. Bind off. With crochet hook, work an edge of sc up fronts and around collar edge. Ch 1, do not turn, but working from left to right, work 1 backwards sc in each sc.
Sew on buttons. Sew snap to top of fronts.

EMBROIDERY

Trace 2 floral embroidery designs onto tissue tracing paper. Tack tissue to outside points of collar. With green floss, embroider leaves in stem st and lazy daisy st. With blue, embroider 2 flowers in lazy daisy st and with coral, embroider outside flower in lazy daisy st. Embroider flower centers in couching st with gold. Work French knots in all colors.

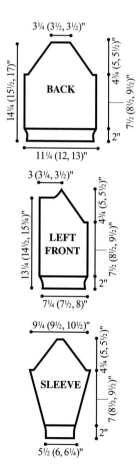

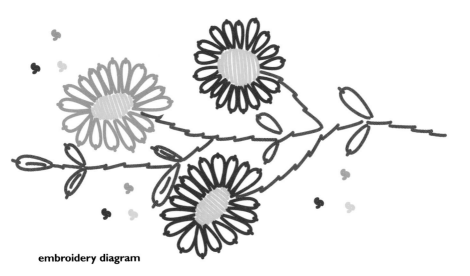

embroidery diagram

Right on course. You'll be the envy of your foursome with these handy beauties, knit in sturdy, comfortable cotton. The modified moss stitch gives them a distinctive texture.

SIZES

▓ Instructions are written for Woman's size 7 (18cm). Changes for sizes 8 and 9 (20 and 23cm) are in parentheses.

MATERIALS

▓ 1 1¾oz/50g ball (each approx 110yd/100m) of Trendsetter Yarn *Elba* each in #934 blue (A) and #932 yellow (B)
▓ One pair size 2 (2.5mm) needles
or size to obtain gauge

GAUGE

28 sts and 40 rows to 4"/10cm over pat st using 2 strands of yarn and size 2 (2.5mm) needles.

Take time to check gauge.

NOTE

Entire glove is worked in pat st using 2 strands of yarn held tog.

PATTERN STITCH

(multiple of 4 sts)
Row 1 (RS) Knit.
Row 2 *P2, k2; rep from * to end.
Row 3 Knit.
Row 4 *K2, p2; rep from * to end.
Rep rows 1-4 for pat st.

LEFT GLOVE

Back

With 2 strands of A, cast on 24 (28, 32)

sts. Work in pat st for 5½ (6, 6½)"/14 (15, 16.5)cm end with row 4 at base of finger.

Index finger

Work 6 (7, 8) sts, turn. Cast on 1 st. Cont in pat st over these 7 (8, 9) sts for 1"/2.5cm. Bind off.

Middle finger

Attach 2 strands of A at base of index finger, cast on 1 st and work across next 6 (7, 8) sts, turn. Cast on 1 st at beg of next row and cont in pat st over these 8 (9, 10) sts for 1"/2.5cm. Bind off.

Ring finger

Work as for middle finger.

Little finger

Attach 2 strands of A at base of ring finger. Cast on 1 st and work as for index finger over 7 (8, 9) sts.

Palm

With B, work as for back.

Thumb

Beg at base, with 2 strands of A, cast on 2 sts. Work in pat st, inc 1 st each side every other row, 7 (7, 8) times—16 (16, 18) sts. Work even until piece measures 3½ (3¾, 4)"/9 (9.5, 10)cm. Bind off.

FINISHING

Sew palm and back tog, seaming all along little finger, then sewing at index finger for 1"/2.5cm from lower edge, leaving 2½ (2¾, 3)"/6.5 (7, 7.5)cm open for thumb and seaming to top. Sew thumb into opening, then sew all finger and thumb seams.

RIGHT GLOVE

Work as for left glove, reversing placement of fingers and thumb.

BABY BUNNY SLIPPERS
Hop along

No baby shower in the '30s would have been complete without a pair of hand-knit bunny slippers. Knit in basic garter stitch to grow with little feet these adorable shoes feature a separate sewn-on bunny.

SIZE
▨ Instructions are written for infant's size 3-6 months.

KNITTED MEASUREMENTS
▨ Length of sole 4"/10cm
▨ Width of foot 2"/5cm

MATERIALS
▨ 1 1¾oz/50g ball (each approx 175yd/158m) of Koigu Wool Designs *Premium Merino* (wool ①) each in #2231 pink (MC) and #2181 ecru (CC)
▨ Small amount fuchsia embroidery floss
▨ One pair size 2 (2.5mm) needles *or size to obtain gauge*
▨ Stitch holder

GAUGE
28 sts and 60 rows to 4"/10cm over garter st using size 2 (2.5mm) needles.
Take time to check gauge.

FIRST SIDE

With MC, beg at center back seam, cast on 12 sts. Work 9 rows in garter st.
Row 10 (WS) K to last 2 sts, k2tog.
Work first 10 rows once more. Work even until there are 18 ridges (or 36 rows) from beg. Sl these sts to a holder. Work second side as foll: pick up a st in each of the 12 cast-on sts at beg (center of back).
Work 9 rows more in garter st.
Next row (WS) K2tog, k to end. Work these 10 rows once more—10 sts.

Join sides

Next row (RS) K 10 sts from holder, cast on 2 sts for instep, k last 10 sts of second side—22 sts. K 1 row, then cont in St st for 12 rows.
Next row (RS) K1, SKP, k to last 3 sts, k2tog, k1—20 sts. P 1 row. Rep these 2 rows. Bind off 10 sts.

SOLE

Cast on 6 sts. K 1 row.
Next row Inc 1 st at beg and end of row—8 sts. Work even in garter st until there are 16 ridges (or 32 rows) from beg. Inc 1 st each side on next row—10 sts. Work even for 12 ridges (or 24 rows). Bind off 1 st at beg of next 2 rows. K 1 row. Bind off. Block pieces. Sew sole into place at bottom of shoe.

BUNNY HEAD

With CC, cast on 3 sts. Working in garter st, inc 1 st each side every other row 4 times—11 sts. Work even until there are 11 ridges (or 22 rows) from beg.
Next row K4, join a 2nd ball of yarn and bind off the next 3 sts, k to end. Working both sides at once, work even for 8 ridges

(or 16 rows). Bind off 1 st at beg of next 2 rows on each ear. K2tog each side and fasten off last st.

FACING FOR EARS
(make 2)
With MC, cast on 5 sts. K 16 rows. Bind off 1 st at beg of next 2 rows. K2tog and pass the last st over the k2tog. Fasten off. Sew bunny head in place (see photo), sewing down all edges (including ears) With embroidery floss, embroider eyes and nose foll diagram.

A single strand of blue, blended with three contrast shades, orchestrates a lovely tweed medley for this classic raglan mock turtleneck. Quick to knit, this enduring style is as wearable now as it was in the 1960s.

SIZES

Instructions are written for size X-Small. Changes for Small, Medium, and Large are in parentheses.

KNITTED MEASUREMENTS
- Bust 34 (37½, 41, 45)"/86 (95, 104, 114)cm
- Length 23½ (24, 24½, 25½)"/59.5 (61, 62, 65)cm
- Upper arm 12 (13, 14¼, 15)"/30.5 (33, 36, 38)

MATERIALS
- 11 1¾oz/50g balls (each approx 64yd/59m) of Cleckheaton *Merino Supreme* by Plymouth Yarn (wool ④) in #2203 blue (MC)
- 4 balls #2207 brown (A) and #2200 ecru (B)
- 3 balls #2201 camel (C)
- One pair size 13 (9mm) needles *or size to obtain gauge*
- Size 13 (9mm) needle, 16"/40cm long
- Size I/9 (5.5mm) crochet hook

GAUGE

8 sts to 3"/7.5cm and 16 rows to 4"/10cm over St st using size 13 (9mm) needles and 2 strands of yarn held tog.

Take time to check gauge.

Note Work with 2 strands of yarn held tog throughout.

BACK

With 1 strand each of MC and A, cast on 45 (50, 55, 60) sts. Beg with a p row, work in St st until piece measures 8½"/21.5cm from beg, end with a WS row. Cut A and join B. Cont in St st until piece measures 15"/38cm from beg, end with a WS row.

Raglan armhole shaping

Bind off 2 sts at beg of next 2 rows.

Row 1 K1, SKP, k to last 3 sts, k2tog, k1.

Row 2 Purl.

Row 3 Knit.

Row 4 Purl.

Cut B and join C. Rep these 4 rows 2 (1, 0, 0) times more. Then rep rows 1 and 2 for 9 (12, 15, 17) times more—17 (18, 19, 20) sts. Bind off.

FRONT

Work as for back to armhole, end with a WS row.

Raglan armhole shaping

Bind off 2 sts at beg of next 2 rows.

Row 1 KI, SKP, k to last 3 sts, k2tog, k1.

Row 2 Purl.

Row 3 Knit.

Row 4 Purl.

Cut B and join C. Rep these 4 rows 4 (3, 2, 1) times more. Then rep rows 1 and 2 for 2 (5, 8, 12) times more end with a WS row—27 (28, 29, 28) sts.

Neck shaping

K1, SKP, k5, join separate balls of yarns

and bind off center 11 (12, 13, 12) sts, k to last 3 sts, k2tog, k1. Cont to dec 1 st at each armhole edge every other row twice more, AT SAME TIME, dec 1 st at each neck edge every other row twice—3 sts rem each side.

Next row (RS) SK2P. Fasten off.

SLEEVES

With 1 strand each of MC and A, cast on 18 (21, 24, 26) sts. Beg with a p row, work in St st, inc 1 st each side every 8th row 4 times—26 (29, 32, 34) sts. Work until piece measures 8½"/21.5cm from beg, end with a WS row. Cut A and join B. Cont to inc 1 st each side every 8th row 3 times more—32 (35, 38, 40) sts. Work even until piece measures 15"/38cm from beg, end with same row and color stripe as on back at armhole.

Raglan cap shaping

Bind off 2 sts at beg of next 2 rows. Rep rows 1-4 of raglan armhole shaping as for back 4 times. Then rep rows 1 and 2 for 7 (8, 9, 11) times more—6 (7, 8, 6) sts. Bind off.

FINISHING

Block pieces to measurements. Sew raglan sleeves into armholes.

COLLAR

With RS facing and circular needle, and 1 strand each MC and C, pick up and k 50 (54, 58, 56) sts evenly around neck edge. Join and work in rnds of St st (k every rnd) for 6"/15cm. Bind off. Turn collar to out-

side. Sew in place using overcast st, with 1 strand MC worked through each bound-off st. Sew side and sleeve seams. With crochet hook and 1 strand MC and A held tog, work an edge of sc around lower and sleeve cuff edges.

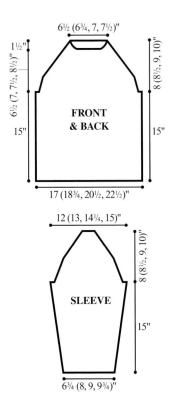

6½ (6¾, 7, 7½)"

1½"

6½ (7, 7½, 8½)"

8 (8½, 9, 10)"

FRONT & BACK

15"

15"

17 (18¾, 20½, 22½)"

12 (13, 14¼, 15)"

8 (8½, 9, 10)"

SLEEVE

15"

6¾ (8, 9, 9¾)"

WOMAN'S ARGYLE ANKLETS
Highland fling

Argyle diamonds are worked in a classic flat pattern around the ankle and along the instep in these traditional woman's socks, as stylish today as they were in the 1940s.

SIZES

Instructions are written for woman's size Medium (8½-9).

MATERIALS

■ 2 1¾oz/50g balls (each approx 227yd/210m) of Schoeller Esslinger/Skacel Collection *Fortissima* (wool ①) in #122 lt grey (A)
■ 1 ball each in #86 blue (B), #123 dk grey (C) and #11 navy (D)
■ Size 1 (2.25mm) straight needles *or size to obtain gauge*
■ 1 set (5) size 1 (2.25mm) dpn
■ Stitch markers
■ Stitch holders
■ Tapestry needle

GAUGE

34 sts and 48 rows/rnds to 4"/10cm over St st using size 1 (2.25mm) needles.
Take time to check gauge.

Notes 1 Cast on and work sock back and forth in rows on two needles to toe. Then, join and work in rnds while shaping toe.
2 Cross lines may be embroidered in duplicate stitch after socks are knit.

CUFF

Beg at top edge with size 1 (2.25mm) straight needle and A, cast on 68 sts. Work in k2, p2 rib for 1½"/4cm, inc 3 sts evenly across last WS row—71 sts.

Beg chart pat

Row 1 (RS) Knit, foll row 1 of argyle chart. Cont to work in St st and foll chart in this way through row 34.

INSTEP

Next row (RS) With A only, k2tog, k16 and sl these 17 sts to a holder for heel. Cont argyle pat across center 35 for instep (working larger diamond in D instead of C) place rem 18 sts on a holder for heel. Cont on 35 sts for instep only, cont diamond with D to end of row 34, then cont diamond with C once more foll rows 1-34. Leave these instep sts on a needle to be worked later.

HEEL

With A, sl 1, k17 sts from first holder, k17 from other heel holder—35 sts. **Next row** Sl 1, purl to end. Cont to work in this way, sl first st of each row, for 32 rows.

Turn heel

Next row (WS) Sl 1, p18, p2tog, p1, turn. **Row 2** Sl 1, k4, SKP, k1, turn. **Row 3** Sl 1, p5, p2tog, p1, turn. **Row 4** Sl 1, k6, SKP, k1, turn. Cont to work in this way, always having 1 more st before dec, and work SKP on RS rows and p2tog on WS rows, until there are 19 sts on heel needle.

GUSSETS AND FOOT

With free needle and A, pick up and k 17

sts along side of heel, k 10 sts of heel to same needle; with another needle, k rem 9 heel sts, pick up and k 17 sts along other side of heel, turn—53 sts. **Next row** P 26 sts of first needle, p 27 sts of 2nd needle. **Next row (RS)** K1, SKP, k to last 3 sts, k2tog, k1. Rep last 2 rows 8 times more— 35 sts. Place these sts on one needle for sole and work back and forth in rows on these 35 sts until there are same number of rows as argyle instep. Sl first 18 sts of foot to one needle, pm to mark beg of rnd (center of sole), sl 17 sts of foot to another needle and sl 6 sts of instep to same needle, sl next 24 sts to another needle, sl last 5 sts of instep to end of first needle—23 sts on *Needles 1 and 3* and 24 sts on *Needle 2.* Rejoin yarn at beg of rnd. **Rnd 1** *K to 1 st before beg of instep, k2tog, rep from * once, k to end—68 sts. Work even in rnds

with A until foot measures 7½"/19cm or 2"/5cm less than desired length from back of heel to end of toe. Make adjustments in length at this point.

Shape toe

Beg at center of sole, place 17 sts on *Needle 1,* 34 sts on needle 2 and 17 sts on *Needle 3.* K to last 3 sts of *Needle 1,* k2tog, k1; on *Needle 2,* k1, SKP, k to last 3 sts of *Needle 2,* k2tog, k1; on *Needle 3,* k1, SKP, k to end. K 1 rnd. Rep last 2 rnds 11 times more—20 sts. Sl first 5 sts of *Needle 1* to *Needle 3.* Hold two needles tog parallel. Weave sts tog using Kitchener stitch.

FINISHING

Block socks lightly. With tapestry needle and B, embroider lines in duplicate st foll chart. Sew instep to sock foot.

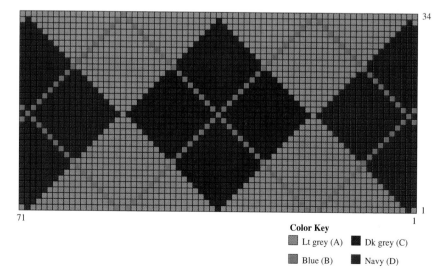

34

71

1

1

Color Key
- Lt grey (A)
- Dk grey (C)
- Blue (B)
- Navy (D)

Ear flaps and tasselled ties add to the charm of this fitted '50s ski cap. Knit in cozy wool, it features a dramatic sloping rib and cable pattern.

SIZES
▥ Directions are for size Medium.

MATERIALS
▥ 1 1¾oz/50g ball (each approx 184yd/170m) of GGH/Muench *Merino Soft* (wool ②) in #38 pink
▥ One pair size 3 (3mm) needles *or size to obtain gauge*
▥ Size 3 (3mm) circular needle, 16"/40cm long
▥ One set (4) size 3 (3mm) dpn
▥ Size C/2 (2.5mm) crochet hook
▥ Cable needle
▥ Stitch marker

GAUGE
28 sts and 32 rows/rnds to 4"/10cm over St st using size 3 (3mm) needles.
Take time to check gauge.

STITCH GLOSSARY
6-st RC
S1 next 3 sts to cn and hold to *front*, k3, k3 sts from cn.

EAR FLAPS
Beg at lower edge with straight needles, cast on 3 sts. Work in St st, inc 1 st each side every other row 9 times—21 sts. Work even until piece measures 4"/10cm from beg, end with a WS row. Work 2nd ear flap in the same way, end with a RS row. On same needle, cast on 32 sts, then k across the sts on first piece—74 sts.

Beg cable pat
Row 1 (WS) Purl.
Row 2 P4, [k6, p8, k8, p8] twice, k6, p4.
Row 3 Inc 1 st in first st, k3, [p6, k8, p8, k8] twice, p6, k3, inc 1 st in last st.
Row 4 P5, [k6, p8, k8, p8] twice, k6, p5.
Row 5 Inc 1 st in first st, k4, [p6, k8, p8, k8] twice, p6, k4, inc 1 st in last st.
Row 6 P6, [6-st RC, p8, k8, p8] twice, 6-st RC, p6.
Row 7 Inc 1 st in first st, k5, [p6, k8, p8, k8] twice, p6, k5, inc 1 st in last st.
Row 8 P7, [k6, p8, k8, p8] twice, k6, p7.
Row 9 Inc 1 st in first st, k6, [p6, k8, p8, k8] twice, p6, k6, inc 1 st in last st—82 sts. Cast on 68 sts—150 sts.
Next row (RS) *K8, p8, k6, p8; rep from * to end. Change to circular needle, join and work in rnds. Place marker for end of rnd and sl marker every rnd. When there are too few sts for circular needle, change to dpn.
Rnd 1 *K8, p3, p2tog, p3, k6, p8; rep from * around—145 sts.
Rnds 2 and 3 *K8, p7, k6, p8; rep from * around.
Rnd 4 *K8, p7, 6-st RC, p3, p2tog, p3; rep from * around—140 sts.
Rnds 5 and 6 *K8, p7, k6, p7; rep from * around.
Rnd 7 *K3, k2tog, k3, p7, k6, p7; rep from * around—135 sts.
Rnds 8 and 9 *K7, p7, k6, p7; rep from * around.

Cont as established, working a 6-st RC every 8th rnd, AT SAME TIME, dec 1 st every 3rd rnd in first purl-panel, 2nd purl-panel and the knit-panel alternately as before (5 sts dec'd on every dec rnd) 6 times more or until 105 sts rem. Then work dec rnd every other rnd until 30 sts rem. Then cont in St st only, dec 5 sts every other rnd until 15 sts rem. Work even for 1½"/4cm. Cut yarn and draw through rem sts. Fasten off.

FINISHING

Block lightly. With crochet hook, work 2 rnds of sc around outer edges.

CORDS

(make 2)

With crochet hook and 2 strands of yam, make a ch 16"/40cm long. Sl st in each ch across. Fasten off. Sew one cord to bottom of each flap. Make another cord 7"/18cm long and sew to top of cap.

TASSELS

Wind yarn 25 times around a 2½"/6.5cm piece of cardboard. Make 3 tassels and attach to cords.

LACE STOLE

Evening wrapture

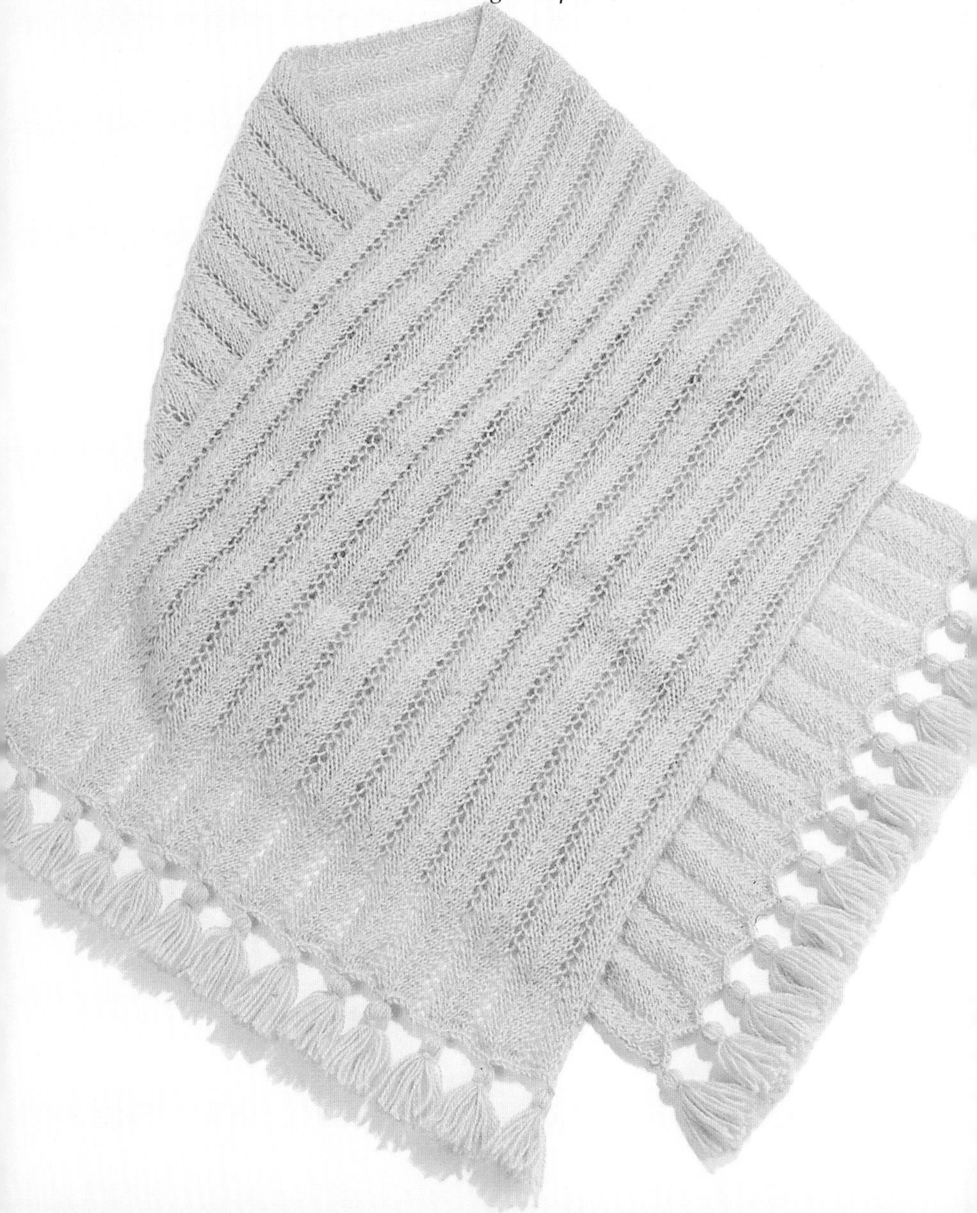

Very Easy Very Vogue

In the 1950s, as summer evenings turned cool, the lightweight lacy stole was *de riguer*. This luxurious version with tasselled trim is knit in an easy rib.

KNITTED MEASUREMENTS
■ Approx 23½" x 72"/59.5cm x 183cm (without fringe)

MATERIALS
■ 6 2½oz/70g balls (each approx 220yd/ 203m) of Lion Brand Yarn Co. *Imagine* (acrylic/mohair ④) in #186 yellow
■ One pair size 9 (5.5mm) needles *or size to obtain gauge*

GAUGE
22 sts and 18 rows to 4"/10cm over lace pat (after blocking) using size 9 (5.5mm) needles.
Take time to check gauge.

LACE PATTERN
(multiple of 9 sts plus 3)
Row 1 K1, k2tog, k3, *yo, k3, k3tog, k3; rep from * to last 6 sts, yo, k3. k2 tog, k1.
Row 2 K1, p4, *yo, p8; rep from * to last 6 sts, yo, p5, k1.
Rep rows 1 and 2 for lace pat.

STOLE
Beg at lower edge, cast on 129 sts. Work in lace pat until piece measures 72"/ 183cm. Bind off.

FINISHING
Lightly block piece to measurements.
Tassels
(make 28)
Cut a piece of cardboard 3"/7.5cm long. Wind one strand of yarn 24 times around cardboard. Tie tightly at one end and slip yarn from cardboard. Wind a single strand 5 times around about ½"/1.5cm from top and tie securely. Cut loops at bottom and trim. Sew tassels along each end to center of each pat point.

Cable vision

Simple '60s chic styling is accented with elementary bubble cables. This basic, timeless shell is given modern definition in a lightweight yarn with a sensual, brushed finish.

SIZES

Instructions are written for size Small. Changes for sizes Medium and Large are in parentheses.

KNITTED MEASUREMENTS

■ Bust 35 (39, 43)"/89 (99, 109)cm
■ Length 21 (21¾, 22½)"/53 (55, 57)cm

MATERIALS

■ 5 (6, 6) 1¾oz/50g balls (each approx 135yd/125m) of Rowan Yarns *Kid Soft* (wool/mohair/nylon ④) in #750 tan
■ One pair size 9 (5.5mm) needles *or size to obtain gauge*
■ Size I/9 (5.5mm) crochet hook
■ One ⅝"/15mm buttons
■ Cable needle

GAUGE

21 sts and 24 rows to 4"/10cm over pat st using size 9 (5.5mm) needles.
Take time to check gauge.

PATTERN STITCH

(multiple of 11 sts plus 3)
Row 1 (RS) P3, *k8, p3; rep from * to end.
Row 2 K3, *p8, k3; rep from * to end.
Row 3 Rep row 1.
Row 4 Rep row 2.
Row 5 P3, *sl next 2 sts to cn and hold to *front*, k2, k2 from cn, sl next 2 sts to cn and hold to *back*, k2, k2 from cn, p3; rep from * to end.
Row 6 Rep row 2.
Row 7 Rep row 1.
Row 8 Rep row 2.
Row 9 P 3, *sl next 2 sts to cn and hold to *back*, k2, k2 from cn, sl next 2 sts to cn and hold to *front*, k2, k2 from cn, p3; rep from * to end.
Row 10 Rep row 2.
Rep rows 1-10 for pat st.

BACK

Cast on 91 (102, 113) sts. Work in pat st until piece measures 12½ (13 13½)"/32 (33, 34)cm from beg.

Armhole shaping

Bind off 4 (6, 7) sts at beg of next 2 rows, 2 sts at beg of next 0 (0, 4) rows, dec 1 st each side every other row 4 (7, 7) times— 75 (76, 77) sts. Work even until armhole measures 4½ (4¾, 5)"/11.5 (12, 12.5)cm.

Back opening

Next row (RS) Work 37 (38, 38) sts, join a 2nd ball of yarn and bind off 1 (0, 1) st, work to end. Work both sides at once until armhole measures 7½ (7¾, 8)"/19 (19.5, 20.5)cm.

Shoulder shaping

Bind off 7 sts from each armhole edge twice, 8 sts once. Bind off rem 15 (16, 16) sts each side for neck.

FRONT

Work as for back, omitting back opening, until armhole measures 5½ (5¾, 6)"/14 (14.5, 15)cm, end with a WS.

Neck shaping

Next row (RS) Work 27 sts, join a 2nd ball of yarn and bind off center 21 (22, 23) sts, work to end. Working both sides at once, dec 1 st at each neck edge every other row 5 times, AT SAME TIME, when same length as back, shape shoulders as for back.

FINISHING

Block pieces to measurements. Sew shoulder and side seams. With crochet hook, work an edge of sc around armhole edges. Work an edge of sc around neck and back neck opening, working a ch-6 button loop at top of right back. Sew on button opposite button loop.

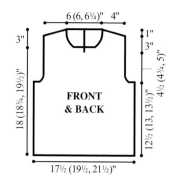

6 (6, 6¼)" 4"

3"

1"
3"

18 (18¾, 19½)"

FRONT & BACK

12½ (13, 13½)"

4½ (4¾, 5)"

17½ (19½, 21½)"

BOY'S TWO-PIECE SUIT

Simply ducky

Get your ducks in a row! Traditional '40s fashion dictates a two-piece ensemble, complete with drawstring pants, a fine-knit gauge, and an adorable little motif.

SIZES
■ Instructions are written for size 2. Changes for size 3 are in parentheses.

KNITTED MEASUREMENTS
Sweater
■ Chest 22½ (24½)"/57 (62)cm
■ Length 13 (14)"/33 (35.5)cm
■ Upper arm 9 (9½)"/23 (24)cm

Pants
■ Length 11 (12)"/28 (30.5)cm
■ Hip 13½ (14½)"/34 (37)cm

MATERIALS
■ 5 (6) 1¾oz/50g balls (each approx 189yd/175m) of Dale of Norway *Baby Wool* (wool ①) in #5703 lt. Blue (MC)
■ 1 ball each in #0010 white (A), #2317 yellow (B) and #5726 dk blue (C). Small amount black yarn.
■ One pair size 3 (3mm) needles OR SIZE TO OBTAIN GAUGE
■ Four ⅜"/10mm buttons

GAUGE
30 sts and 40 rows to 4"/10cm over St st using size 3 (3mm) needles.
Take time to check gauge.

SWEATER
BACK
With A, cast on 85 (93) sts. K2 rows.
Beg 2-color rib
Row 1 (RS) K1 MC, p1 A; rep from *, end with k1 MC. **Row 2** P1 MC, *k1 A, p1 MC; rep from * to end. Rep these 2 rows until piece measures 1½ (2)"/4 (5)cm from beg, dec 1 st on last WS row—84 (92) sts. Change to MC and cont in St st until pieces measure 8½ (9)"/21.5 (23)cm from beg.
Armhole shaping
Bind off 4 (5) sts at beg of next 2 rows. Dec 1 st each side every other row 2 (3) times—72 (76) sts. Work 1 row even. **Next row (RS)** K 34 (36) sts (for right side). Leave rem sts unworked. **Next row** Cast on 4 sts (for center placket), p to end—38 (40) sts. Work even until armhole measures 4 (4½)"/10 (11.5)cm.
Shoulder shaping
Bind off 7 (8) sts from shoulder edge twice, 8 (7) sts once. Bind off rem 16 (17) sts for neck.
Left side
Rejoin yarn to work left side sts and cast on 4 sts. Work as for right side on 38 (40) sts reversing shoulder shaping.

FRONT
Work as for back until pieces measure 3½"/9cm from beg.
Beg duck chart
Next row (RS) K 7 (11) MC, work duck chart sts 1-26 once, then sts 1-44 once, k7

(11) MC. Cont to foll chart in this way through row 24. Then cont with MC only as for back, until armhole measures 2¾ (3¼)"/7 (8)cm.

Neck shaping

Next row (RS) K29 (30), join another ball of yarn and bind off center 14 (16) sts. Work to end. Cont to work both sides at once, dec 1 st at each neck edge every other row 7 times. When armhole measures 4 (4½)"/10 (11.5)cm, bind off 7 (8) sts from each shoulder edge twice, 8 (7) sts once.

SLEEVES

With A, cast on 67 (73) sts. K 2 rows then work in 2-color rib until piece measures 1¼"/3cm from beg, dec 1 st on last WS row—66 (72) sts. Change to MC and cont in k1, p1 rib (with MC only) for 4 rows more. Then cont in St st until piece measures 3¼ (4)"/8 (10)cm from beg.

Cap shaping

Bind off 4 (5) sts at beg of next 2 rows. Dec 1 st each side every other row 11 (13) times. Bind off 3 sts at beg of next 8 rows. Bind off rem 12 sts.

COLLAR

(make 2 pieces)

With A, cast on 55 (59) sts. K 2 rows, then work in 2-color rib until piece measures 2½"/6cm. Bind off.

FINISHING

Block pieces to measurements. Sew shoulder seams. Sew sleeves into armholes. Sew side and sleeve seams. With crochet hook and MC, work an edge of sc along right and back placket opening. Work sc in same way along left back opening, working four ch-5 buttonloops evenly spaced. Sew on buttons opposite buttonloops. Sew to collar pieces around neck edge. With A, work an edge of sc along straight edge of back and front collar points. With C, embroider feet and bills foll chart. With black, embroider eyes on ducks.

PANTS

(make 2 pieces)

Beg at waistband of pants, with MC, cast on 86 (94) sts. Work in k2, p2 rib for 4 rows. **Next (eyelet) row (RS)** *K2, yo, p2tog, rep from *, end k2. Cont in rib until piece measures 1"/2.5cm from beg. Then cont in St st for 2 rows. **Next row** Knit, inc 8 sts evenly spaced—94 (102) sts. Cont in St st, inc 1 st each side every 12th row 4 times—102 (110) sts. Work even until piece measures 6 (7)"/15 (18)cm from beg. **Next row** K1, k2tog, k to last 3 sts, SKP, k1. Rep this row every other row 5 times more—90 (98) sts.

Short row shaping

Next row (RS) K1, k2tog, k35 (37), turn. P 1 row. **Next row** K1, k2tog, k 29 (31), turn. P 1 row. **Next row (RS)** K1, k2tog, k23 (25) turn. P 1 row. Cont to work 6 less sts at end of RS rows until 7 (9) sts rem at end of last short row shaping. P 1 row.

Next row (RS) K1, k2tog, k across all sts to last 3 sts, SKP, k1. Work other short row shaping at opposite edge to correspond, working SKP, k1 on RS rows and beg short rows on p rows. When all short rows and decs are completed, 76 (84) sts rem. Cast on 5 (6) sts at beg of next 2 rows and work in 2-color rib for 1½"/4cm. With A, k 1 row, then bind off knitwise with A.

CROTCH INSERT

With MC, cast on 20 (24) sts. Work in St st inc 1 st at beg of every k row 5 times— 25 (29) sts. Work even until piece measures 2½ (2¾)"/6.5 (7)cm from beg.

Next row (RS) K to last 2 sts, k2tog. P 1 row. Rep last 2 rows 4 times more. Bind off rem 20 (24) sts.

FINISHING

Block pieces to measurements. Fold 2 pieces in half lengthwise and seam 2 pieces along center front and back seams. Sew crotch insert into pants. With 3 strands of MC, make a 30"/76cm twisted cord. Knot ends and thread through eyelet row of pants.

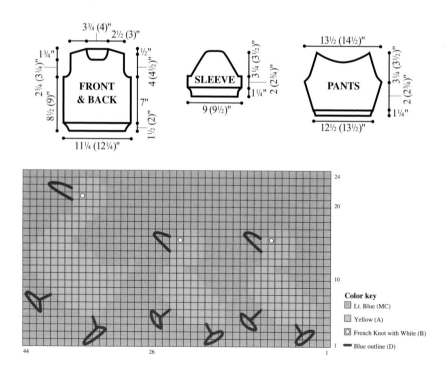

Color key
- Lt. Blue (MC)
- Yellow (A)
- French Knot with White (B)
- Blue outline (D)

Graphic two-color headband and mittens trace their pattern roots to Nordic snowflake and grid motifs. As up to date now as they were in the 1940s, the defined mitten shape and snug-fitting headband are perennial ski-wardrobe staples.

SIZES
■ To fit Woman's size Small.

KNITTED MEASUREMENTS
■ Headband circumference 16"/40.5cm
■ Hand width 6½"/16.5cm

MATERIALS
■ 1 1¾oz/50g balls (each approx 131yd/120m) of Knit One, Crochet Two *Creme Brulee DK* (wool ④) each in #101 white and #909 black
■ One pair size 6 (4mm) needles *or size to obtain gauge*
■ 1 set (4) size 6 (4mm) dpn
■ Size E/4 (3.5mm) crochet hook
■ Stitch holders

GAUGE
22 sts and 28 rows to 4"/10cm over St st and chart pat using size 6 (4mm) needles. *Take time to check gauge.*

Note
We have shown two different color ways, one with black as MC and white as CC, and the other vice versa.

HEADBAND
With MC, cast on 9 sts.
Row 1 (RS) *P1, k1; rep from *, end p1. Cont in rib, inc 1 st each side every other row 6 times—21 sts. Cast on 4 sts at beg of next WS row and rib across. Sl sts to a holder. Make a 2nd piece in same way, only beg with a WS row as foll: *K1, p1; rep from *, end k1. When there are 21 sts, cast on 4 sts at beg of next RS row.
Next row (RS) Rib 25 sts, then separately with MC, cast on 41 sts for front of headband and k these sts, then rib 25 sts—91 sts. Cont to work in rib on first and last 25 sts and work in St st and rows 1-21 of chart on 41 sts. When chart is completed, bind off.

FINISHING
Block lightly. Sew center back seam. With crochet hook and MC, work an edge of sc around all edges of headband.

LEFT MITTEN
With MC, cast on 41 sts.
Set up row (RS) K21 (for chart pat), *p1, k1; rep from * to end. Beg with row 1 (WS row) of chart, work 20 sts in rib as established, 21 sts foll chart. Cont to work in this way for 16 rows more, inc 1 st at beg of last WS row—42 sts. Then work 32 sts, sl 8 sts to holder for thumb and cast on 8 sts to replace these sts, k2. Work even through row 51 of chart.

Top shaping
Next row (RS) SKP, work to last 2 sts of chart, SK2P, k to last 2 sts, k2tog. Rep this row every other row 6 times more—14 sts. Divide sts on 2 needles and weave tog using Kitchener st.

THUMB
With MC and dpn, pick up and k 8 sts from cast-on sts, pick up 1 st at side of thumb, work across 8 sts from holder, pick up 1 st at side of thumb—18 sts.

Divide sts on 3 needles and work in rnds of St st for 2"/5cm.

Next rnd [K2tog, k7] twice. K 1 rnd.
Next rnd [K2, k2tog] 4 times. K 1 rnd.
Next rnd [K2tog] 6 times. Cut yarn and draw through rem 6 sts. Fasten off.

RIGHT MITTEN

Work to correspond to left mitten, only beg with 20 sts in rib and end with 21 sts of chart. For thumb placement, k2, then sl 8 sts to holder for thumb and cont as for left mitten. For top shaping, work dec rnd as foll:

Next (dec) rnd (RS) SKP, work to 1 st before 21-st chart, SK2P, work to last 2 sts of chart, k2tog. Finish as for left mitten.

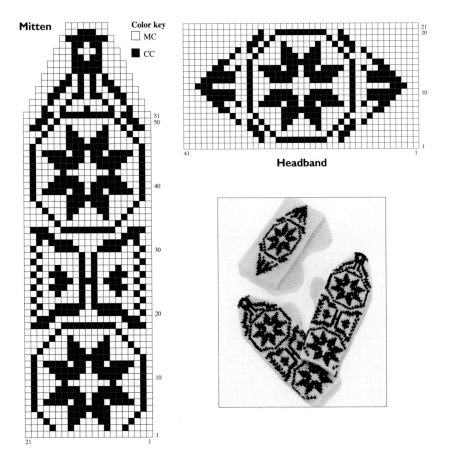

Mitten

Color key
☐ MC
■ CC

Headband

INFANT'S FUR-TRIMMED OUTFIT

Baby's first fur

Double-layered knitted fabric makes this cute little outfit extra warm for winter babies. Add a luscious sewn-on faux-fur trim for 1930s retro-styling that's very up to the minute. Try working the lining in a contrast color for reversible wear.

SIZES

Instructions are written for size 3-6 months. Changes for sizes 12 and 18 months are in parentheses.

KNITTED MEASUREMENTS

- Chest 22 (25½, 27)"/56 (65, 68.5)cm
- Length 11 (12¾, 14)"/28 (32.5, 35.5)cm
- Upper arm 7 (7½, 8)"/18 (19, 20)cm

MATERIALS

- 6 (7, 8) 1¾oz/50g balls (each approx 189yd/175m) of Garnstudio/Aurora Yarns Baby-ull (wool ③) in #6 pink
- One pair size 5 (3.75mm) needles OR SIZE TO OBTAIN GAUGE
- Size D (3mm) crochet hook
- 3yd/3m of 2"/5cm white *Mokuba* fake fur trim
- 1yd/1m of ⅝"/15mm white *Mokuba* silk ribbon

Mokuba New York, 55 West 39th Street, New York, NY 10018
Phone: (212) 869-8900

- Matching sewing thread and yarn needle

GAUGES

- 21 sts and 40 rows to 4"/10cm over seed st using size 5 (3.75mm) needles
- 21 sts and 42 rows to 4"/10cm over garter st using size 5 (3.75mm) needles. *Take time to check gauges.*

SEED STITCH

(over an odd number of sts)
Row 1 (RS) K1, *p1, k1; rep from * to end.
Rep row 1 for seed st.

Note All 3 pieces are made with a double-layer of knitting with the seed st on the outside and garter st on the inside. Even and neat seaming will make these pieces reversible.

JACKET

Outside piece
Beg at lower back edge, cast on 53 (59, 65) sts. Work in seed st for 7½ (9, 10)"/19 (23, 25.5)cm from beg.
Beg sleeve
Cast on 30 (31, 37) sts at beg of next 2 rows—113 (121, 139) sts. Work even in seed st until sleeve measures 3½ (3¾, 4)"/9 (9.5, 10)cm.
Back neck shaping
Next row (RS) Work 46 (49, 57) sts, join another ball of yarn and bind off center 21 (23, 25) sts, work to end. Cont to work both sides at once, work 5 rows even. Then, inc 1 st at inside (neck) edge on next row then every other row 16 (17, 17) times more—63 (67, 75) sts each side. Work even, if necessary, until sleeve cuff edge measures 7 (7½, 8)"/18 (19, 20)cm. Bind off 30 (31, 37) sts at beg of next 2 rows for sleeve seams and cont on rem 33 (36, 38)

sts each side until same number of rows as back to lower edge. Bind off.

LINING PIECE

Work as for outside piece, ONLY work in garter st instead of seed st.

FINISHING

Block pieces to measurements. Sew side and sleeve seams of each piece. Sew all edges of lining and outside piece tog. Baste fur trim around front and neck edges trimming to fit. Sew trim in place with sewing thread, keeping sts small and even, as foll: Sew one edge of fur to inside edge of garment all around the front and neck edges. Fold fur piece over edge to right side of garment and sew in place. Sew trim around cuffs in same way, seaming at inside edge. Cut two 10"/25.5cm lengths of ribbon and sew to fronts under trim.

CAP

(one size)

OUTSIDE PIECE

Cast on 59 sts. Work in seed st for 4"/10cm.

Next row (RS) Work 21 sts, k2tog, work 13 sts, k2tog, work 21 sts.

Next row Bind off 21 sts, work seed st to end. Rep last row once—15 sts. Cont in seed on these 15 sts for 4"/10cm.

Next row [Work 2 sts, dec 1 st] 3 times, work 3 sts—12 sts. Bind off. Block lightly. Sew sides of 4"/10cm piece over 15 sts to the 21 bound-off sts to form back of cap.

LINING

Work as for outside piece, ONLY work in garter st instead of seed st. Finish as for outside piece. Holding pieces tog, work an edge of sc along lower edge of cap, drawing in slightly to fit neck, if necessary.

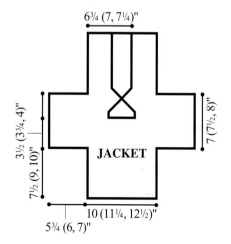

6¾ (7, 7¼)"

3½ (3¾, 4)"

7½ (9, 10)"

7 (7½, 8)"

JACKET

10 (11¼, 12½)"

5¾ (6, 7)"

Sew on fur as for jacket. Cut two 14"/35.5cm lengths of ribbon and two 3"/7.5cm pieces of fur trim. Fold fur in half to form a pompom and sew to end of ribbon ties.

Note

Fur pompons can also be purchased from Mokuba New York, (see address in Materials section.) Sew on ties at lower edge of cap.

BOOTIES

(one size)

OUTSIDE PIECE

Beg at lower (sole) edge, cast on 45 sts. Work in seed st for 1½"/4cm.

Dec row (RS) Work seed st over 18 sts, k2tog, pm, k5, pm, k2tog, work seed st to end. Work even for 1 row. Cont to dec 2 sts every other row (each side of center 5 sts) 6 times more—31 sts. Work even until piece measures 4¼"/11cm from beg. Bind off.

FINISHING

Work as for outside piece in garter st. Block pieces lightly. Fold in half at center of 5-st instep and sew tog cast-on edge for sole. Sew back seam. With crochet hook, work an edge of sc around top of bootie. Sew fur around top of bootie as for jacket. Sew edges of fur trim tog at seam.

GIRL'S THREE-PIECE SET

Cuddly soft

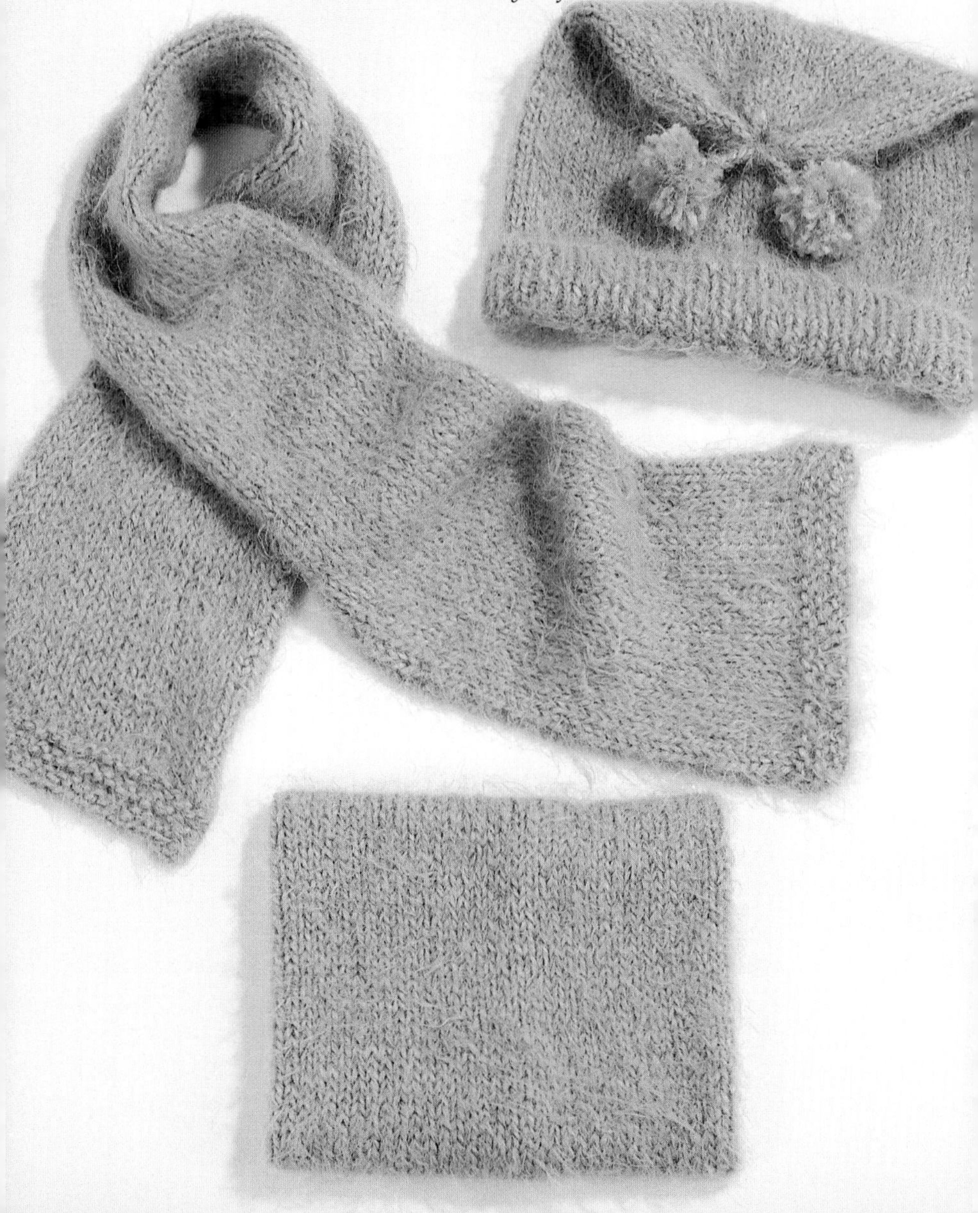

Luxury yarn in vintage rose, with the softness and feel of faux fur, gives these adorable little-girl accessories their special appeal. Designed in the 1930s, they can be worn separately or together for a stunning ensemble.

KNITTED MEASUREMENTS
- Scarf approx 5½" x 36"/14cm x 91cm
- Head circumference 18"/45.5cm

MATERIALS
- 5 1¾oz/50g balls (each approx 90yd/83m) of Berroco, Inc. *Furz* (nylon/acrylic/wool ⑤) in #3862 pink
- One pair each sizes 8 and 10 (5 and 6mm) needles *or size to obtain gauge*
- Size G/6 (4mm) crochet hook

GAUGES
- 20 sts and 26 rows to 4"/10cm over St st using size 8 (5mm) needles.
- 17 sts and 21 rows to 4"/10cm over St st using size 10 (6mm) needles.
Take time to check gauge.

SCARF

With larger needles, cast on 24 sts. Work in garter st for 1"/2.5cm.

Next row (RS) Knit.

Next row K1, p22, k1.

Rep these 2 rows until piece measures 35"/88.5cm from beg. Work in garter st for 1"/2.5cm. Bind off.

HAT

With smaller needles, cast on 90 sts. Work in k1, p1 rib for 10 rows.

Next row K 1 row for turning ridge.

Cont in k1, p1 rib for 6 rows more.

Next row Then work in St st for 5"/12.5cm.

Next (dec) row [K8, k2tog] 9 times—81 sts. Work 3 rows even.

Next (dec) row [K7, k2tog] 9 times—72 sts. Work 3 rows even.

Next (dec) row [K6, k2tog] 9 times—63 sts. Work 3 rows even.

Next (dec) row [K5, k2tog] 9 times—54 sts. Work 3 rows even.

Next (dec) row [K4, k2tog] 9 times—45 sts. Work 3 rows even.

Next (dec) row [K3, k2tog] 9 times—36 sts. Work 3 rows even.

Next (dec) row [K2, k2tog] 9 times—27 sts. Cut yarn and draw through rem sts. Fasten tightly.

FINISHING

Block to measurements. Sew back seam.

Pompoms

With crochet hook, ch 14. Attach a 1"/2.5cm pompom to each end of ch and sew to top of hat.

MUFF

With smaller needles, cast on 70 sts. Work in St st for 20"/50.5cm. Bind off.

FINISHING

Block piece. Fold in half lengthwise and sew side edge tog to form inside seam. Sew doubled cast on and bound off edges tog. Fold inside seam to center and block muff flat.

SACQUE, CAP & BOOTIES

Peaches 'n cream

The stylish baby was shown off in a classic knitted ensemble. In keeping with past traditions, this finely knit baby set features a pretty butterfly stitch pattern and is trimmed with matching ribbon.

SIZES

Instructions are written for size 3-6 months. Changes for size 12 months are in parentheses.

KNITTED MEASUREMENTS

▓ Chest 22½ (24)"/57 (61)cm
▓ Length 9 (10)"/23 (25.5)cm
▓ Upper arm 8 (8¾)"/20.5 (22)cm

MATERIALS

▓ 3 (4) 1¾oz/50g balls (each approx 262yds/240m) Patons® *Kroy 3 Ply* (wool ①) in #333 lt green
▓ One pair size 2 (2.75mm) needles *or size to obtain gauge*
▓ Size D/3 (3mm) crochet hook
▓ Three ⅜"/10mm buttons
▓ 2 yds/1.9m ⅜"/10mm wide ribbon
▓ Cable needle

GAUGE

33 sts and 40 to 4"/10cm over pat st using size 2 (2.75mm) needles.
Take time to check gauge.

PATTERN STITCH

multiple of 6 sts

Row 1 (WS) Purl. **Row 2** *Pass in front on next 2 sts and k 3rd st in front, k first and 2nd sts and sl from needle, k3; rep from * to end. **Row 3** Purl. **Row 4** *K3, sl next st to cn and hold to *front*, k2, k1 from cn; rep from * to end. Rep these 4 rows for pat st.

SACQUE—BODY

Beg at lower edge, cast on 186 (198) sts. Work in pat st until piece measures 5½ (6)"/14 (15)cm from beg, end with row 4 of pat.

Separate for back and fronts

Next row P 45 (48) for left front and sl to holder; bind off 4 sts for armhole and p until there are 88 (94) sts for back, sl these sts to a holder; bind off 4 sts for armhole and work to end—45 (48) sts for right front.

RIGHT FRONT

Row 1 (RS) Knit. **Row 2** Bind off 2 sts, p to end. **Row 3** Work row 2 of pat st. **Row 4** Bind off 2 sts, p to end—41 (44) sts. **Row 5** Work row 4 of pat st. **Row 6** Purl. **Row 7** Work row 2 of pat st. **Row 8** Purl. **Row 9** Knit. **Row 10** Purl. Rep these 10 rows (omitting armhole bind-offs) for yoke pat until armhole measures 2½ (3)"/6.5 (7.5)cm, end with a WS row.

Neck shaping

Next row (RS) Bind off 12 sts (neck edge), work to end. Cont in 10-row pat as before until armhole measures 3½ (4)"/9 (10)cm. Bind off 29 (32) sts for shoulder.

LEFT FRONT

Rejoin yarn and work to correspond to right front, reversing all shaping.

BACK

Work as for right front, working 10-row yoke pat and binding off 2 sts at beg of next 4 rows for armholes—80 (86) sts. Work even until armhole measures 3¼ (3¾)"/8 (9.5)cm.

Neck shaping

Next row (RS) Work 29 (32) sts, join 2nd ball of yarn and bind off center 22 sts, work to end. Work both sides at once until armhole measures 3½ (4)"/9 (10)cm. Bind off.

SLEEVES

Cast on 42 (48) sts. Work in St st for 8 rows. **Next row (RS)** *K2, inc 1 st in next st; rep from *13 (15) times more—56 (64) sts. P 1 row. **Next row (RS)** Knit, inc 8 sts evenly spaced—64 (72) sts. Work even in pat st until piece measures 6½ (7½)"/16.5 (19)cm from beg.

Cap shaping

Working 10-row yoke pat, bind off 3 sts at beg of next 2 rows, 2 sts at beg of next 22 (18) rows, 3 sts at beg of next 2 (6) rows. Bind off rem 8 (12) sts.

FINISHING

Block pieces to measurements. Sew shoulder seams. Sew sleeves into armhole. Sew sleeve seams.

Crochet edge

With RS facing and crochet hook, work 1 sc *ch 3, 1 dc in next st, skip 2 sts, sc in next st; rep from * around edge of sacque and cuffs. Sew 3 buttons to left front to correspond to crochet edge loops. Cut a 14"/35.5cm length of ribbon. Tie in a bow and sew to right front edge

CAP (one size)

Beg at face edge, cast on 120 sts. Work in pat for 6¾"/17cm. Bind off 42 sts at beg of next 2 rows—36 sts. Cont in pat st for 4¾"/12cm or until straight piece fits along bound-off sts of each side. Bind off.

FINISHING

Block lightly. Sew straight piece to sides of bound-off sts of front. Fold back face edge (cast-on row) for ½"/1.5cm and work crochet edge on jacket through 2 thicknesses.

Lower edge

Working along lower edge of cap, work 1 sc evenly along lower edge. Ch 1, turn. Next (eyelet) row 1 sc, ch 5, *skip 3 sc, 1 dc in next sc, ch 2; rep from * across. Ch 1, turn. Work crochet edge along eyelet row as before. Fasten off. Cut a 34"/86cm length of ribbon and draw through eyelet row.

BOOTIES (one size)

Beg at top edge, cast on 42 sts. Work in pat st for 3"/7.5cm **Next row (RS)** Work 15 sts and sl to a holder; work next 12 sts; sl rem 15 sts on holder. Work on 12 instep sts for 2¼"/6cm. Sl sts to a holder.

Beg foot

With RS facing, work across 15 sts from first holder, pick up and k 11 sts along side of instep, k12 sts from instep, pick up and k 11 sts along other side of instep, work 15 sts from last holder—64 sts. Work in garter st for 17 rows more. **Next row** K1, k2tog, k28, k2tog, k to last 3 sts, k2 tog, k1. K 1 row. Bind off.

Block piece. Fold bootie in half and sew sole seam along bound-off edge, sew back seam. Work sc crochet edge around top. Cut a 10"/25cm length of ribbon and tie in a bow. Sew to center of bootie.

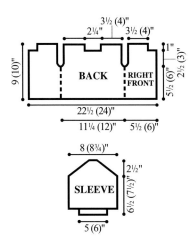

NOTES

NOTES

RESOURCES

Write to the yarn companies listed below for purchasing and mail-order information.

AURORA YARNS
PO Box 3068
Moss Beach, CA 94038-3068

BAABAJOES WOOL CO.
PO Box 260604
Lakewood, CO 80226

BERROCO, INC.
14 Elmdale Rd.
PO Box 367
Uxbridge, MA 01569

BROWN SHEEP CO., INC.
100662 County Road 16
Mitchell, NE 69357

CLASSIC ELITE YARNS
300A Jackson Street
Bldg. 5
Lowell, MA 01852

CLECKHEATON
distributed by
Plymouth Yarn

DALE OF NORWAY, INC.
N16 W23390 Stoneridge Drive
Suite A
Waukesha, WI 53188

FILATURA DI CROSA
distributed by
Tahki•Stacy Charles, Inc.

GARNSTUDIO
distributed by
Aurora Yarns

GGH
distributed by
Muench Yarns

GRIGNASCO
distributed by
JCA

JAEGER HANDKNITS
5 Northern Blvd.
Amherst, NH 03031

JCA
35 Scales Lane
Townsend, MA 01469

KIC2, LLC
2220 Eastman Ave. #105
Ventura, CA 93003

KOIGU WOOL DESIGNS
R. R. #1
Williamsford, ON N0H 2V0
Canada

LANE BORGOSESIA
PO Box 217
Colorado Springs, CO 80903

LION BRAND YARN CO.
34 West 15th Street
New York, NY 10011

MUENCH YARNS
285 Bel Marin Keys Blvd.
Unit J
Novato, CA 94949-5724

NATURALLY
distributed
S. R. Kertzer, Ltd.

PATONS®
PO Box 40
Listowel, ON N4W 3H3
Canada

PLYMOUTH YARN
PO Box 28
Bristol, PA 19007

REYNOLDS
distributed by
JCA

ROWAN YARNS
5 Northern Blvd.
Amherst, NH 03031

S. R. KERTZER, LTD.
105A Winges Road
Woodbridge, ON L4L 6C2
Canada

SCHOELLER ESSLINGER
distributed by
Skacel Collection, Inc.

SKACEL COLLECTION, INC.
PO Box 88110
Seattle, WA 98138-2110

STAHL WOLLE
distributed by
Tahki•Stacy Charles, Inc.

TAHKI•STACY CHARLES, INC.
1059 Manhattan Ave.
Brooklyn, NY 11222

TAHKI YARNS
distributed by
Tahki•Stacy Charles, Inc.

TRENDSETTER YARNS
16742 Stagg Street
Suite 104
Van Nuys, CA 91406

WOOL PAK YARNS NZ
distributed by
Baabajoes Wool Co.

*Write to US resources for
mail-order availability
of yarns not listed.*

AURORA YARNS
PO Box 28553
Aurora, ON L4G 6S6

BERROCO, INC.
distributed by
S. R. Kertzer, Ltd.

CLASSIC ELITE YARNS
distributed by
S. R. Kertzer, Ltd.

CLECKHEATON
distributed by
Diamond Yarn

DIAMOND YARN
9697 St. Laurent
Montreal, PQ H3L 2N1
and
155 Martin Ross, Unit #3
Toronto, ON M3J 2L9

**ESTELLE DESIGNS &
SALES, LTD.**
Units 65/67
2220 Midland Ave.
Scarborough, ON M1P 3E6

FILATURA DI CROSA
distributed by
Diamond Yarn

GARNSTUDIO
distributed by
Aurora Yarns

GRIGNASCO
distributed by
Estelle Designs & Sales, Ltd.

KOIGU WOOL DESIGNS
R. R. #1
Williamsford, ON N0H 2V0

NATURALLY
distributed by
S. R. Kertzer, Ltd.

PATONS®
PO Box 40
Listowel, ON N4W 3H3

ROWAN
distributed by
Diamond Yarn

S. R. KERTZER, LTD.
105A Winges Rd.
Woodbridge, ON L4L 6C2

SCHOELLER ESSLINGER
distributed by
Diamond Yarn

---

*Not all yarns used in this
book are available in
the UK. For yarns not
available, make a
comparable substitute or
contact the US manufacturer
for purchasing and
mail-order information.*

ROWAN YARNS
Green Lane Mill
Holmfirth
West Yorks HD7 1RW
Tel: 01484-681881

SILKSTONE
12 Market Place
Cockermouth
Cumbria CA13 9NQ
Tel: 01900-821052

**THOMAS RAMSDEN
GROUP**
Netherfield Road
Guiseley
West Yorks LS20 9PD
Tel: 01943-872264

VOGUE KNITTING VINTAGE KNITS

Editor-in-Chief
TRISHA MALCOLM

Art Director
CHRISTINE LIPERT

Executive Editor
CARLA S. SCOTT

Managing Editor
SUZIE ELLIOTT

Contributing Editor
DARYL BROWER

Instruction Writer
MARI LYNN PATRICK

Technical Illustration Editor/
Page Layout
CHI LING MOY

Instructions Editor
KAREN GREENWALD

Instructions Coordinator
CHARLOTTE PARRY

Knitting Coordinator
JEAN GUIRGUIS

Yarn Coordinator
VERONICA MANNO

Editorial Coordinators
KATHLEEN KELLY
MICHELLE LO

Photography
BRIAN KRAUS, NYC
BOBB CONNORS
TERRANCE CARNEY
Photographed at Butterick Studios

Stylists
MONICA GAIGE-ROSENSWEIG
MELISSA MARTIN

Production Managers
LILLIAN ESPOSITO
WINNIE HINISH

■

President and CEO, Butterick® Company, Inc.
JAY H. STEIN

Executive Vice President and Publisher, Butterick® Company, Inc.
ART JOINNIDES